Midlothian *our* library

PRESERVE

Sweet & savoury recipes

hamlyn

Preparation/cooking times do not include time for sterilizing jars etc.

Note

Both metric and imperial measurements have been given in all recipes.
Use one set of measurements only, and not a mixture of both.

Standard level spoon measurements are used in all recipes.
1 tablespoon = one 15 ml spoon
1 teaspoon = one 5 ml spoon

The Department of Health advises that eggs should not be consumed raw. This book contains dishes made with lightly cooked eggs. It is prudent for vulnerable people such as pregnant or nursing mothers, invalids, the elderly, babies and young children to avoid uncooked or lightly cooked dishes made with eggs. Once prepared, these dishes should be kept refrigerated and used promptly.

This book includes dishes made with nuts and nut derivatives. It is advisable for people with known allergic reactions to nuts and nut derivatives and those who may be potentially vulnerable to these allergies, such as pregnant and nursing mothers, invalids, the elderly, babies and children, to avoid dishes made with nuts and nut oils. It is also prudent to check the labels of pre-prepared ingredients for the possible inclusion of nut derivatives.

Ovens should be preheated to the specified temperature – if using a fan-assisted oven, follow the manufacturer's instructions for adjusting the time and temperature.

Vegetarians should look for the 'V' symbol on a cheese to ensure it is made with vegetarian rennet. There are vegetarian forms of Parmesan, feta, Cheddar, Cheshire, Red Leicester, dolcelatte and many goats' cheeses.

First published in Great Britain in 2005 by Hamlyn,
a division of Octopus Publishing Group Ltd
2–4 Heron Quays, London E14 4JP

ISBN 0 600 61142 6
EAN 9780600611424

A CIP catalogue record for this book is available from the British Library.

Printed and bound in China

10 9 8 7 6 5 4 3 2 1

Contents

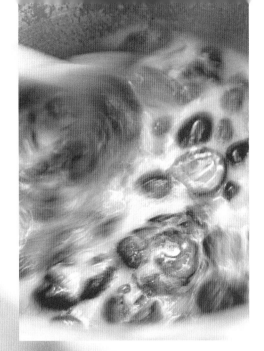

Introduction

There is nothing quite so delicious as a spoonful of home-made jam with a thick slice of crusty bread. Making your own preserves conjures up nostalgic thoughts of a bygone age and taking time to prepare and cook fruit-packed jams, tangy marmalades or spicy chutneys can be a welcome break from the stresses and strains of modern living. Preserves are rewarding to give to friends, too. Who could resist a jar of passion fruit and lime curd, bottled figs with vanilla, or a bottle of sloe gin?

If you haven't tried making preserves before, seize the moment now with these easy-to-follow, step-by-step recipes and their clear, helpful pictures. More experienced cooks will find new flavour combinations and twists on old favourites.

Basic equipment

Preserving pans This is probably the largest pan a cook will ever use. It should be at least 25 cm (10 inches) in diameter and 11 cm (4½ inches) deep. Its wide diameter is essential for good evaporation and to give the jam room to boil without boiling over. As a guide, never fill it more than half full. It has a hinged handle that can be locked upright to move it safely from the cooker and laid flat against the top of the pan during cooking, plus a second, ear-shaped, handle that is useful when the pan needs to be tipped, to spoon out the last remains of jam.

Preserving pans are available in aluminium, stainless steel, enamel or

copper. Choose one with a thick base to reduce the chances of the jam burning. Copper pans heat up quickly, but unless they are lined with aluminium they are unsuitable for making chutney as the vinegar reacts with the metal. Some pans come with a lid, but if you do not have one you could improvise with a large baking sheet or piece of foil folded over the edge of the pan.

For bottling fruit, syrups or cordials the depth of the pan is important and a deep stock pot is ideal. Allow enough room between the jars or bottles so that the heat can penetrate. The pan should be deep enough to cover the containers or at least to come up to the necks. Keep the base of the jars away from direct heat by putting a small wire rack in the bottom first. This will ensure that the contents heat up evenly.

Sugar thermometer When jams or jellies are coming up to set it can be difficult to judge how long the process will take – a quick look at a sugar thermometer soon makes it obvious and ensures good results every time.

A thermometer is crucial when bottling fruits and making fruit cordials because there are no visual clues such as bubbles breaking

on the surface or a skin forming on a saucer to indicate when the process is complete.

Before you use the thermometer check that it is reading accurately by putting it into a small pan of cold water. Bring the water slowly to the boil and boil for 2 minutes. The thermometer should read 100°C (212°F). Never plunge a thermometer straight into boiling liquids. If treated with care, thermometers will last a lifetime.

Jelly bag As jellies are made with unpeeled, uncored fruits, straining through a bag is crucial for crystal clear juice. The closer the mesh of the cloth of the jelly bag, the finer the finished jelly or cordial will be. Traditionally made of white cotton flannel or felt, jelly bags are now more commonly made from fine nylon mesh, but both kinds work in the same way. First suspend the bag from a specially designed frame or by tying string to the loops and suspending it from an upturned stool or eye-level cupboard handle and place a large bowl beneath so that the bottom of the bag is just above the bowl. Scald the bowl with boiling water and empty it, then fill the bag with the cooked fruit and cooking liquid. Leave undisturbed for 3–4 hours or overnight so that the juice runs through the bag freely and the fibres of the bag trap any particles of fruit. Avoid squeezing the bag or the juice will go cloudy.

After use, wash the bag well in boiling water – do not use detergent or washing-up liquid – and dry thoroughly before storing. If you make preserves only occasionally, you can improvise by lining a large fine nylon sieve with a new fine cotton mesh dishcloth or a double layer of muslin.

Spoons In the initial stages of cooking a jam or chutney, use a long-handled wooden spoon for stirring, to keep your hand away from the hot preserve. If possible, buy one with a notch in the handle that fits on the side of the pan to stop it sliding into the preserve.

At the end of cooking, remove any scum with a flat stainless steel perforated spoon with small holes. Don't skim during cooking otherwise you will waste a lot of your preserve.

Funnels A jam funnel reduces spills down the sides of the jars and helps eliminate scalds when potting jams, chutneys and jellies. Always made of metal to withstand the high temperatures of just-cooked jams or chutneys, jam funnels usually measure 12–15 cm (5–6 inches) across the top with a 4–5 cm (1½–2 inch) tube.

For filling bottles with cordials, syrups or liqueurs, a small plastic funnel is ideal. When making liqueurs, choose a funnel with a tube about 1.5 cm (¾ inch) wide, so that sugar as well as liquid can be poured down.

Jars, bottles and tops Recycle jam jars for jams, jellies, marmalades, fruit butters and chutneys; heavy glass vinegar and oil bottles for cordials; or wide-necked, screw-topped glass spirit bottles for fruit liqueurs. Bottling requires purpose-bought bottling jars with rubber rings or gaskets and spring or screw lids. The most commonly sold are glass Le Parfait jars with metal spring clasps and bright orange rubber rings. They are widely available and come in a range of sizes.

If you have the older-style Kilner jars with gold rings and glass lids, or Fowler Lee jars with black metal clips, check them over carefully. If the inside coating on the metal rings is scratched do not use them, as the acid from the fruit will react with it and spoil the flavour of the preserve.

Check all jars carefully before use and throw away any with cracks or chips – this is especially important when heat processing. Soak the rubber rings for Le Parfait jars in warm water for 10–15 minutes before use so that they fit snugly on to the top of the jar. If the jam jars do not come with lids, cover jams and jellies with cellophane tops and secure in place with rubber bands.

The importance of sterilizing

Hygiene is really important when
preserving and especially when potting
the finished preserves. Make sure jars and
bottles are well washed, rinsed with hot
water and dried, then sterilized in a warm
oven for 10 minutes; where indicated use
while hot or warm. Alternatively, jam jars
and Le Parfait jars may be sterilized on a
standard wash cycle in a dishwasher, and
filled while still warm if indicated. Ensure
they are dry before filling them. You should
also sterilize jam funnels and screw-topped
lids, if using. Preparation times given in the
recipes do not include sterilizing.

Covering preserves

How you cover the finished preserve is
crucial. For jams, jellies, marmalades and
chutneys, always press a disc of waxed
paper (available in packs with cellophane
jam pot covers and labels), waxed side
down, on to the surface of the preserve
while still very hot. Add a cellophane cover
and secure with a rubber band, or add a
sterilized screw-topped lid and leave to
cool. As the preserve cools, the heat kills
any bacteria or mildew spores from the air
trapped between the lid and the waxed
disc. Chutneys, which also require a waxed
disc, and pickles must have a good plastic-
coated airtight lid – not just to keep the
bacteria out, but to stop the vinegar
evaporating. Label each jar to identify its
contents and add the date when made. If
the preserve has to stand for fruit to settle
before potting, then it is best, after adding
the waxed disc, to wait until the preserve is
cold before sealing.

Storage

The key to successful and long storage of
preserves is a cool, dark place away from
direct sunlight. Choose a kitchen cupboard
well away from the boiler, cooker or
window, or use the cupboard under the
stairs. If the storage place is too warm then
the jam will shrink, too light and the
colour will fade, and any damp will make
the preserve mouldy. See recipes for
individual storage times. Refrigerate
preserves after opening.

How to make the perfect jam, jelly and marmalade

Choosing the fruit

Always choose fruit that is firm and ripe or just under-ripe for maximum pectin content (see below). Cut out any blemishes, then weigh the fruit. Depending on the type of fruit, either rinse with water and pat dry with kitchen paper or wipe clean.

Which sugar is best?

Sugar is a vital factor in the setting process of preserves and should make up between 55–70% of them. Lump, preserving or granulated sugars are best when making jams, jellies or conserves as they dissolve to a colourless liquid and do not affect the natural colour of the fruits. Preserving sugar dissolves faster than the others and produces less scum, but it is more expensive. Golden granulated or soft light brown sugar may be added to marmalade for a darker, stronger-flavoured finish. Unless a specific sugar is indicated in the recipe, use lump, preserving or granulated.

What is pectin?

Pectin is a natural gum-like substance found in varying amounts in the seeds, pips, cores and skins of fruit. When fruits are crushed and warmed the pectin is released and mixes with the natural acids in the fruit to produce a jelly-like set. Fruits low in pectin are very often mixed with others that are high, such as strawberries with redcurrants or rhubarb and apple. Freshly squeezed lemon juice is often added to fresh strawberry jam, allowing 2 tablespoons for every 1 kg (2 lb) of fruit. Citric acid, available in powdered form from the chemist, can also be added, allowing 1 teaspoon per 1 kg (2 lb) of fruit. Commercially made pectin or preserving sugar with added pectin and citric acid may also be used.

Pectin levels

High Cooking apples, crab apples, cranberries, black, red and white currants, damsons, under-ripe gooseberries, grapes, grapefruit, japonicas, lemons, limes, oranges, firm acid plums, quinces, rowanberries.
Medium Fresh apricots, early blackberries, greengages, loganberries, morello or may duke cherries, mulberries, ripe plums, under-ripe raspberries, dessert apples.
Low Sweet cherries, elderberries, medlars, melons, peaches, pears, pineapples, rhubarb, strawberries.

Initial cooking

All fruits require cooking before the sugar is added and timings depend on the fruits used – from 10–15 minutes for delicate berry fruits and up to 45–60 minutes for cooking apples or citrus fruits. The volume of water needed also varies, with more needed for fruits that require longer cooking times.

Adding sugar

Always warm the sugar when adding it to hot liquid so that it dissolves quickly. Adding cold sugar will make the temperature of the jam drop and by the time it has risen once more, you may be in danger of overcooking the jam. To warm sugar, tip it into a roasting tin and warm for 10 minutes in a preheated oven, 160–180°C (325–350°F), Gas Mark 3–4.

Testing for a set

Once the sugar has been added to cooked fruit and dissolved, a set should almost be reached within 10–20 minutes of rapid boiling. Longer than that and the jam will be very dark and overcooked. There are several ways of testing whether a preserve has reached setting point:

Flake test After 10–15 minutes, stir the jam well with a wooden spoon, then turn the spoon in the hand to cool it a little and allow the jam to drop from it. If the jam is ready, it will partly set on the spoon and the drops will run together to form flakes that will fall cleanly off the spoon. If the jam runs freely off the spoon back into the pan, it is not ready.

Saucer test After 10–15 minutes, turn off the heat, then spoon a little of the preserve on to a small saucer. Put it into a cold place or the freezer for 2–3 minutes, then run a finger through the preserve. If it wrinkles and the indentation made by your finger remains, the preserve is ready. If not, turn the heat back on and continue to boil the fruit, checking at 5-minute intervals until it reaches setting point.

Using a thermometer

Clip a sugar thermometer over the side of the preserving pan when you first begin to cook the jam so that the thermometer and jam warm up together. As the jam will be hotter in the centre of the pan, stir well before checking the thermometer. Setting point is 105°C (221°F).

Yield

As a very rough guide, the finished jam or jelly will make between 1½–2 times the amount of sugar used.

Know your preserves

Conserves are jams with a slightly softer set and are generally made with a mix of whole and crushed fruits. Serve spread on bread or toast, or add to fruit desserts.

Chutneys are a cross between a pickle and a jam with a sweet and sour taste. Like jam, they require boiling, but all the ingredients are added to the pan at once and then simmered until thick, rather than until a set is reached. Serve with savouries such as cheese, cold meats or grilled sausages.

Crystallized fruit are fruits soaked in sugar syrup over 10–14 days, then dried and rolled in sugar. They are most often served as petits fours.

Glacé fruit are similar to crystallized fruit, but are finished by dipping the fruit into a thick sugar syrup for a glossy finish.

Jams are made from crushed fruit and should have a slightly runnier set than a jelly.

Jellies are clear preserves made from cooking diced fruit, with its pips, seeds, skins and cores, in just enough water to cover. It is then strained to make a clear juice and boiled with sugar until set firm. Spread on bread or toast. Rowan, quince or cranberry jellies are traditional.

Fruit butters are made from fruit purées cooked with sugar until the consistency of thick cream. Serve with thickly sliced bread, toasted muffins or crumpets.

Fruit cheeses are made in the same way as fruit butters, but are cooked until very thick. Serve with cheeses as part of a cheese course.

Fruit curds usually contain butter and eggs and are cooked in a double boiler or in a bowl set over a pan of simmering water. As they contain eggs they must be stored in the refrigerator and used within one month.

Marmalades are a jam made exclusively from citrus fruits. The rinds may be pared from the fruit and then mixed with the squeezed juice, or the fruits may be cooked whole and then cut into fine shreds. Serve at breakfast, spread on thick toast.

Mincemeat is not minced meat at all, but made with minced dried fruits and grated or cooked apples and flavoured with sugar, alcohol and spices. It is traditionally served at Christmas as a filling for small or large tarts.

Pickles are made from vegetables or fruits and preserved in sweetened vinegar. Most often, vegetables are pickled raw after soaking in salt. Serve with cold cuts, salads and cheese.

Relishes are of Indian origin and may be cooked or uncooked; they are more highly spiced than a chutney. Serve to accompany curries, cold meats or barbecued food.

Bottling

Bottling is an easy way of preparing summer fruits, but timing and controlling the heat are essential. There are four methods of bottling: in the oven, in a pressure cooker, the slow and the quick bath – the slow water and oven method being the most popular. The strength of syrup that you use will depend on both personal taste and the fruit that you are bottling. Peaches, for example, are best in a heavy syrup, whereas plums are best in a light to medium syrup. The lighter the syrup, the better the appearance of the fruit, so if bottling as gifts use a really light syrup.

Light syrup	125 g (4 oz) sugar
	600 ml (1 pint) water
Medium syrup	250–300 g (8–10 oz) sugar
	600 ml (1 pint) water
Heavy syrup	375–500 g (12 oz–1 lb) sugar
	600 ml (1 pint) water

To make the syrup, boil the sugar and water together, stirring continuously, until the sugar has dissolved. If the syrup is slightly cloudy, strain through very fine muslin.

For the slow water bath

1 Pour cold syrup over cold fruit in sterilized jars. When tightening the jar lids it is important that some air can escape or the jar could explode during processing – Le Parfait or Fowler Lee jars have metal clasps that give slightly and these lids can be completely tightened. Kilner jars, however, do not have any give and you should tighten and then loosen the lids slightly.

2 Stand the jars on a wire rack in the bottom of a large deep pan. Submerge the jars in cold water or, if the pan is not deep enough, fill to reach the neck of the jars.

3 Put a sugar thermometer into the pan and slowly heat the water over the course of 1 hour to a temperature of 55°C (130°F), then continue heating for 30 minutes to a temperature of 74–87.5°C (165–190°F) – the lower temperature for fragile berry fruits, the higher for larger denser pears.

Maintain this temperature for a further 10–30 minutes (10 minutes for berry fruits and rhubarb, 15 minutes for halved peaches, plums and apricots, and 30 minutes for halved pears). Keep an eye on the temperature, adjusting the heat so that it rises slowly. If the heat is too rapid the fruit will be overcooked and will lose colour. It sounds complicated, but as long as you are in the kitchen while the heating process is going on, it needs only a quick glance at the thermometer and clock to check that everything is going as it should.

4 Ladle some of the water out of the pan, then, using oven gloves, carefully lift the jars out. Using a cloth, tighten the lids then leave to cool. Check the seal before storing.

In the oven

1 Following the recipe, pour boiling syrup over cold fruit in sterilized jars. Loosely screw or fasten the lids.

2 Stand the jars on a baking sheet, spaced well apart, and cook in the centre of a preheated oven, 150°C (300°F), Gas 2, for 15–40 minutes, depending on the size and firmness of the fruit, or until the fruit just begins to rise in the syrup. Small to medium jars are best for this method. With large jars, the top layer of fruit may discolour as it takes a long time for the heat to penetrate the whole jar. Make sure that you leave at least 5 cm (2 inches) between the jars so that the heat can circulate. This method is not suitable for fruits that require longer cooking times, such as pears or quinces.

Cordials, syrups and liqueurs

Keeping the colour

To capture the true colour of the fruit make sure that you do not overcook it. Soft berries such as raspberries, strawberries and currants are best cooked in a bowl over a pan of simmering water, but can also be cooked slowly and very gently in a pan. Cooking apples, which require much longer cooking times, are the exception. If mixing with other fruits, add these towards the end of cooking to preserve the intensity of colour.

In the clear

A good jelly bag is essential when making fruit cordials or syrups. Suspend the jelly bag over a bowl and scald (see page 5). Add the cooked fruit and leave to slowly drip through for 2–3 hours. Resist the temptation to squeeze the bag as this will spoil the finished syrup.

Measure the cold juice into a large pan and add 250–375 g (8–12 oz) granulated sugar for each 600 ml (1 pint) of juice. Cook over a low heat, stirring continuously, until the sugar has completely dissolved. If there is any scum, carefully skim off with a slotted spoon, or strain the hot syrup through a nylon jelly bag, fine sieve or sieve lined with a square of muslin.

Filling the bottles

Remove any plastic inside the bottle tops as these will melt during heating. Sterilize bottles and screw-tops or corks before use.

Using a small sterilized funnel, fill the bottles to within 2.5–4 cm (1–1½ inches) of the tops and loosely screw the tops on, or press the corks in, to allow for expansion during cooking. Tighten after heat processing. If using corks, seal when cool with melted paraffin wax.

The importance of heat

Heating or sterilizing the bottles of fruit syrup for cordial is essential for long storage. The slow water bath gives the best results.

1 Stand a small wire rack in the bottom of a large deep pan and put the bottles, slightly spaced apart, on the rack. Wedge folded pieces of newspaper between the bottles so that they do not fall over or knock together, then fill the pan with cold water to reach the necks of the bottles.
2 Put a sugar thermometer into the pan and slowly heat the water over the course of 1 hour to 77°C (170°F), then maintain the temperature for 20–30 minutes depending on the size of the bottles. Ladle some of the water out of the pan, then, using tongs, carefully lift the bottles out on to a wooden board and, using a cloth, seal tightly. Leave to cool overnight, then store in a cool, dark place.

Other ways to preserve foods

Using alcohol

Transform a bottle of cheap gin with the addition of sloes, or brandy with apricots, peaches, plums or damson, or vodka with strawberries. Leave small fruits whole, but pierce them so that the fruit juices soak into the alcohol; slice larger fruits. As a general rule, add two-thirds alcohol and one-third sugar. Set aside for at least 1 month or up to 1 year. Strain and decant into a bottle before serving. Serve the soaked fruits on their own with cream, ice cream, trifles or meringues. Sloes are the only fruit that may not be eaten afterwards.

Steeping in vinegar

Transform plain red or white wine vinegar, malt or distilled vinegar into an aromatic seasoning with the addition of spices or herbs. Steep the flavouring for several weeks, then strain and bottle. Use to pep up meaty casseroles, salad dressings or sauces. Use larger quantities in chunky chutneys, sweet and sour relishes or as a base for pickled fruit and vegetables.

Oil as a preservative

This is a quick way to prepare preserves without any cooking. Simply pack sliced, diced or tiny whole cheeses or olives into sterilized jars with flavourings such as sliced onions, capers, herbs, garlic or pared lemon or orange rind, then cover with olive oil. Tap the jars on a work surface to release any air bubbles, then seal well with screw-topped lids. Store olives at room temperature, cheeses in the refrigerator.

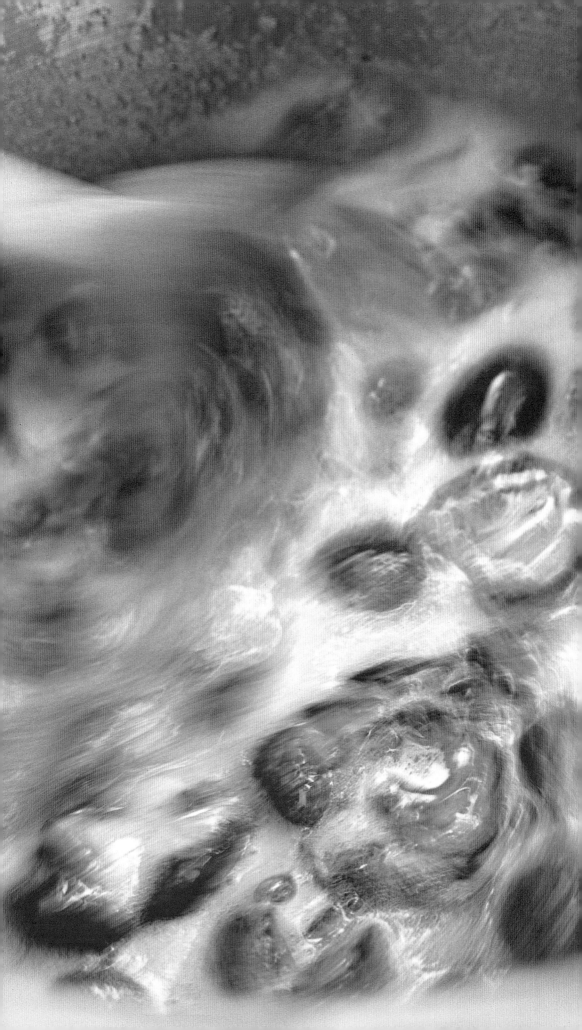

Jams, jellies and conserves *are rewarding and relaxing to make and are the best known of all the preserves. Once you have sampled your own home-made efforts you will be reluctant to go back to shop-bought jams, jellies and conserves. They are not difficult to make, providing you follow the basic guidelines and ensure that all the pectin is fully released during cooking and mixed with the right amount of acid, so that the finished preserve will set successfully.*

Jams are usually made with crushed fruits, while jellies are made with cooked fruits that are then strained, so the whole raw fruit can be chopped roughly, rather than finely, which saves time if you are making large batches. Conserves are a softer-set jam made with a mixture of crushed and whole fruits.

Raspberry and redcurrant jam

If you do not like too many seeds in jam, then cook half the fruit separately and press it through a sieve before adding it to the remaining fruit.

MAKES: about 1.5 kg (3 lb)
PREPARATION TIME: 5 minutes
COOKING TIME: about 1 hour

500 g (1 lb) raspberries
500 g (1 lb) redcurrants
300 ml (½ pint) water
juice of 2 lemons
1 kg (2 lb) sugar

1 Mix the fruit in a large pan and add the water. Bring to the boil, then reduce the heat and cover the pan. Simmer for 20–30 minutes, until the redcurrants are really tender.

2 Add the lemon juice and sugar and stir over a low heat until the sugar has completely dissolved.

3 Increase the heat and bring to the boil, then boil hard to setting point. Remove the pan from the heat and, using a slotted spoon, carefully skim off any scum.

4 Transfer the jam to warm dry jars. Cover the surface of each with a disc of waxed paper, waxed side down, then top with an airtight lid or cellophane cover. Label and leave to cool, then store in a cool, dark place. It will keep for 3–4 months.

Raspberry and redcurrant jam

Blackberry and apple jam
Blackberry and apple jam is delicious on hot buttered toast and in jam tarts, or you can pile it lavishly on the base of a custard tart to create a delicious dessert.

MAKES: about 3.25 kg (7 lb)

PREPARATION TIME: 15 minutes, plus standing

COOKING TIME: 1 hour

1 kg (2 lb) slightly under-ripe blackberries, stalks discarded

1.75 kg (3½ lb) sugar

1 kg (2 lb) cooking apples

300 ml (½ pint) water

juice of 2 large lemons

1 Layer the blackberries in a large bowl with the sugar and leave to stand overnight.

2 Peel, core and slice the apples. Place all the trimmings in a pan and pour in the water. Bring to the boil and boil, uncovered, for about 20 minutes until most of the water has evaporated and the trimmings are pulpy. Press the mixture through a fine sieve into a large pan.

3 Add the apple slices to the pan and pour in the blackberries with all their juice and any undissolved sugar. Heat the mixture gently to simmering point, stirring continuously, for about 10 minutes until the sugar has completely dissolved and the fruit is soft. Add the lemon juice.

4 Bring the jam to the boil and boil hard to setting point. Remove from the heat and, using a slotted spoon, carefully skim off any scum.

5 Transfer the jam to warm dry jars. Cover the surface of each with a disc of waxed paper, waxed side down, then top with an airtight lid or cellophane cover. Label and leave to cool, then store in a cool, dark place. It will keep for 3–4 months.

Rhubarb, orange and ginger jam

The ginger provides this jam with a real zing, which is wonderful with the orange and rhubarb. If you don't like ginger it may be omitted – the jam will be just as delicious.

MAKES: 2.75–3.25 kg (6–7 lb)

PREPARATION TIME: 10 minutes, plus cooling

COOKING TIME: 1¾ hours

1.5 kg (3 lb) trimmed rhubarb, sliced

50 g (2 oz) fresh root ginger, peeled and finely chopped

juice and chopped pared rind of 2 oranges

2 lemons, halved

1.2 litres (2 pints) water

1.75 kg (3½ lb) sugar

1 Put two-thirds of the rhubarb into a large pan and mix in the ginger, orange rind and the juice from the lemons, then add the orange juice and water. Chop the lemon shells and tie them securely in a piece of clean muslin, then add to the pan. Bring the mixture to the boil, reduce the heat and simmer steadily, uncovered, for about 1 hour. The fruit should be reduced by half at the end of the simmering time.

2 Allow the fruit to cool, then remove the muslin and squeeze out all the juices from it into the pan. Add the remaining rhubarb, return the jam to the boil and simmer for 5–10 minutes, until the fruit is soft. Gradually stir in the sugar and continue stirring over a low heat until the sugar has completely dissolved. Bring the jam to the boil once more and boil hard to setting point. Remove the pan from the heat and, using a slotted spoon, carefully skim off any scum.

3 Transfer the jam to warm dry jars. Cover the surface of each with a disc of waxed paper, waxed side down, then top with an airtight lid or cellophane cover. Label and leave to cool, then store in a cool, dark place. It will keep for 3–4 months.

Melon and ginger jam

A delicately flavoured jam that sets firmly. This is delicious served with very thin slices of bread and butter as a mid-morning snack.

MAKES: 1.5 kg (3 lb)

PREPARATION TIME: 10 minutes

COOKING TIME: 1½ hours

1 ripe honeydew melon

500 g (1 lb) cooking apples, roughly chopped

75 g (3 oz) fresh root ginger, peeled and coarsely grated

1.2 litres (2 pints) water

juice of 3 lemons

1 kg (2 lb) sugar

1 Halve the melon, scoop out the seeds and put them into a large pan. Slice the melon into quarters, cut out the flesh and put to one side. Chop all the peel and put it into the pan with the seeds, then add the apples, ginger and water. Bring to the boil, then cover the pan and boil for 30 minutes. Press the mixture through a sieve into a cleaned pan.

2 Chop the reserved melon flesh and add to the sieved liquid in the pan. Cover the pan and simmer for about 15 minutes.

3 Add the lemon juice and sugar and cook over a low heat, stirring continuously, until the sugar has completely dissolved. Bring to the boil and boil hard to setting point. Remove from the heat and, using a slotted spoon, carefully skim off any scum.

4 Transfer the jam to warm dry jars. Cover the surface of each with a disc of waxed paper, waxed side down, then top with an airtight lid or cellophane cover. Label and leave to cool, then store in a cool, dark place. It will keep for 3–4 months.

Pineapple and passion fruit jam

When properly ripe, passion fruit will have wrinkly skins and feel heavy for their size. Their fragrant pulp combines well with the sweet juicy flesh of the pineapple in this fruity jam.

MAKES: about 2 kg (4 lb)
PREPARATION TIME: 15 minutes
COOKING TIME: 2½ hours

1 large ripe pineapple
750 g (1½ lb) cooking apples, roughly chopped
6 passion fruit, cut into quarters
1.2 litres (2 pints) water
1.5 kg (3 lb) sugar
juice of 2 large lemons

1 Peel the pineapple and roughly chop the peel together with any leaves. Put the chopped peel and leaves into a pan with the apples and passion fruit and pour in the water. Bring to the boil, then reduce the heat, cover the pan and simmer for 1 hour.

2 Meanwhile, chop the pineapple flesh, cutting up the hard core more finely than the soft part of the fruit.

3 Press the cooked pulp through a fine sieve, pour the resulting purée back into the pan and add the fresh pineapple. Bring the fruit mixture slowly to the boil, then reduce the heat to a simmer, cover the pan and cook the fruit for 30 minutes or until quite tender.

4 Add the sugar and lemon juice and cook over a low heat, stirring continuously, until the sugar has completely dissolved. Bring to the boil and boil hard to setting point. Remove from the heat and, using a slotted spoon, carefully skim off any scum.

5 Transfer the jam to warm dry jars, cover the surface of each with a disc of waxed paper, waxed side down, then top with an airtight lid or cellophane cover. Label and leave to cool, then store in a cool, dark place. It will keep for 3–4 months.

Chestnut jam with whisky
This jam is delicious simply spread on toast or hot-buttered muffins. Or you could try layering it with yogurt, for a light dessert.

MAKES: 550 g (1 lb 2 oz)
PREPARATION TIME: 15 minutes
COOKING TIME: 50 minutes

625 g (1¼ lb) cooked, peeled chestnuts
1 vanilla pod
375 g (12 oz) soft light brown sugar
2 tablespoons whisky

1 Put the chestnuts and vanilla pod into a heavy-based pan and add enough water just to cover them. Bring to the boil, then reduce the heat, cover the pan and simmer for 30 minutes. Remove the vanilla pod, then strain and reserve the cooking liquid. Purée the chestnuts in a food processor or blender, adding a little of the reserved liquid if necessary, or put them through a food mill.

2 Put the chestnut purée back into the pan. Slice the vanilla pod lengthways and scrape the seeds into the pan. Add the sugar and 75 ml (3 fl oz) of the cooking liquid and stir to blend. Bring to the boil, stirring frequently, and cook for about 5 minutes or until very thick. Remove from the heat and add the whisky.

3 Transfer the jam to a warm dry jar and cover the surface with a disc of waxed paper, waxed side down, then top with an airtight lid or cellophane cover. Label and leave to mature for 2 days in a cool, dark place before using, or store, unopened, for up to 6 months.

Chestnut jam with whisky

Cherry conserve

This delicious conserve is perfect as an accompaniment to a special dessert. Use it to fill a sponge flan, top a creamy vanilla mousse or pour into individual semolina moulds.

MAKES: about 1.5 kg (3 lb)

PREPARATION TIME: 15 minutes

COOKING TIME: 1¼ hours

1 kg (2 lb) sour cherries (Morello or Montmorency), pitted

1 kg (2 lb) sugar

150 ml (¼ pint) brandy or orange liqueur (Cointreau, Curaçao)

1 Put the cherries into a large pan and add the sugar. Pour in the brandy or liqueur and cook over a low heat, stirring continuously, until the sugar has completely dissolved.

2 Bring the fruit to the boil, then lower the heat and simmer gently, uncovered, stirring occasionally, for about 1 hour until it is reduced to about two-thirds of its original volume.

3 Transfer the conserve to warm dry jars. Cover the surface of each with a disc of waxed paper, waxed side down, then top with an airtight lid or cellophane cover. Label and leave to mature in a cool, dark place for about 1 month before using, or store, unopened, for 3–4 months.

Physalis and ginger conserve *A light and delicious conserve, excellent spread on plain or fruit breads, croissants and scones and in Victoria sponge sandwiches.*

MAKES: 1 kg (2 lb)

PREPARATION TIME: 10 minutes, plus standing

COOKING TIME: 25 minutes

500 g (1 lb) physalis

500 g (1 lb) preserving sugar

7 cm (3 inch) piece of fresh root ginger, peeled and finely chopped

1 small lemon, halved

3 tablespoons water

1 Discard the paper-like petals from the physalis, then rinse the berries in a colander.

2 Put the sugar into a large heavy-based pan with the berries, ginger and lemon halves. Add the water and cook over a low heat, stirring continuously, for 10 minutes until the sugar has completely dissolved. Increase the heat and bring to the boil, then boil to setting point.

3 Remove the pan from the heat and, using a slotted spoon, carefully skim off any scum and remove and discard the lemon shells. Leave the conserve to stand for 15 minutes to allow the fruit to settle.

4 Stir the conserve once again, then transfer to warm dry jars. Cover the surface of each with a disc of waxed paper, waxed side down, then leave until cold. Top the cold jars with airtight lids or cellophane covers. Label and store in a cool, dark place. It will keep for 3–4 months.

Gooseberry and almond conserve
The almonds add texture to the gooseberries in this conserve. Serve it as a topping on simple baked apples or as a fruit sauce with apple pies, rice puddings and ice cream.

MAKES: about 1.5 kg (3 lb)

PREPARATION TIME: 15 minutes

COOKING TIME: 1 hour

1 kg (2 lb) gooseberries, topped and tailed

125 g (4 oz) blanched almonds, halved

juice of 3 lemons

300 ml (½ pint) water

1 kg (2 lb) sugar

1 Put the gooseberries into a pan with the nuts, lemon juice and water. Bring to the boil, then reduce the heat and cover the pan. Simmer for 20 minutes until the fruit is soft.

2 Add the sugar and cook over a low heat, stirring continuously, until the sugar has completely dissolved. Increase the heat and bring to the boil, then boil, uncovered, for 20 minutes, stirring occasionally, until thickened to a heavy syrup.

3 Transfer the conserve to hot jars and cover the surface of each with a disc of waxed paper, waxed side down, then top with an airtight lid or cellophane cover. Label and leave to cool, then store in a cool, dark place. It will keep for 3–4 months.

Strawberry and Champagne conserve *This timeless favourite has been given the star treatment with the addition of Champagne. Serve with thickly sliced bread and butter, warm scones, crumpets or toast.*

MAKES: 2.25 kg (5 lb)

PREPARATION TIME: 10 minutes, plus standing

COOKING TIME: 20 minutes

1.5 kg (3 lb) strawberries, hulled

1.5 kg (3 lb) preserving sugar with added pectin

150 ml (¼ pint) or 1 glass dry Champagne or sparkling white wine

1½ teaspoons citric acid

1 Pick over the strawberries and discard any bruised or very soft ones. Halve or quarter them depending on their size, then put half of them into a large pan and roughly crush with a potato masher. If the strawberries are difficult to mash, warm them a little in the pan and then try again.

2 Add the sugar, the remaining strawberries, the Champagne or wine and citric acid and heat gently for 10 minutes, stirring continuously, until the sugar has completely dissolved.

3 Increase the heat and boil rapidly for 5–10 minutes, testing at 5-minute intervals until a set is reached. Using a slotted spoon, carefully skim off any scum, then leave the conserve to stand for 15 minutes to allow the fruit to settle.

4 Transfer the conserve to warm dry jars. Cover the surface of each with a disc of waxed paper, waxed side down, and leave until cold. Top the cold jars with airtight lids or cellophane covers. Label and store in a cool, dark place. It will keep for 6–12 months.

Strawberry and Champagne conserve

Crab apple jelly
This slightly sharp jelly is not only good on hot buttered toast but it also makes the perfect accompaniment to ham, gammon steaks or roast pork.

MAKES: about 3 lb (1½ kg)
PREPARATION TIME: 10 minutes, plus straining
COOKING TIME: 2¼ hours

2 kg (4 lb) crab apples, roughly chopped
1.2 litres (2 pints) water
juice of 2 lemons
4 cloves
sugar

1 Put the crab apples into a pan, add the water and lemon juice, then stir in the cloves. Bring to the boil, then lower the heat and cover the pan. Simmer for about 1½ hours, until reduced to a pulp.

2 Allow to cool slightly, then strain the mixture overnight through a jelly bag suspended over a large bowl.

3 The next day, measure the resulting juice and pour it into a large pan. Add 500 g (1 lb) of sugar for each 600 ml (1 pint) of liquid and cook over a low heat, stirring continuously, until the sugar has completely dissolved. Increase the heat and bring to a rapid boil, then boil hard to setting point. Using a slotted spoon, carefully skim off any scum.

4 Transfer the jelly to warm dry jars. Cover the surface of each with a disc of waxed paper, waxed side down, then top with an airtight lid or cellophane cover. Label and leave to cool, then store in a cool, dark place. It will keep for 3–4 months.

Rose hip and apple jelly
Choose firm, just-ripe rose hips for making jelly. If you are using windfall apples, make sure any bruised or damaged parts are removed before weighing.

MAKES: about 2 lb (1 kg)
PREPARATION TIME: 20 minutes, plus straining
COOKING TIME: 50 minutes

500 g (1 lb) rose hips
600 ml (1 pint) water
1 kg (2 lb) cooking apples, roughly chopped
sugar
lemon juice

1 Put the rose hips with 300 ml (½ pint) of the water into a pan, then bring to the boil, cover the pan and simmer for 45–50 minutes. Put the apples with the remaining water into another pan, bring to the boil, cover the pan and simmer until reduced to a pulp.

2 Allow both pans of fruit to cool, then strain each one overnight in its own jelly bag suspended over a large bowl.

3 Mix together the resulting juices, measure and pour into a clean pan. Add 500 g (1 lb) sugar and the juice of 1 lemon for each 600 ml (1 pint) of juice, then stir over a low heat until the sugar has completely dissolved. Increase the heat and boil hard to setting point. Using a slotted spoon, carefully skim off any scum.

4 Transfer the jelly to warm dry jars. Cover the surface of each with a disc of waxed paper, then top with an airtight lid. Leave to cool, then store in a cool, dark place. It will keep for 3–4 months.

Grape and port jelly

This is a soft-setting jelly, which should be stored in a cool place. It has an excellent flavour and will complement any home-made ice cream, vanilla mousse or delicate cheesecake.

MAKES: about 1.5 kg (3 lb)

PREPARATION TIME: 10 minutes

COOKING TIME: 1¾ hours plus overnight straining

1 kg (2 lb) red grapes with stalks, halved

3 lemons, halved

1.8 litres (3 pints) water

about 750 g (1½ lb) sugar

150 ml (¼ pint) port

1 Put the grapes into a large pan with their stalks. Squeeze and reserve the juice from the lemons. Chop the lemon shells and add to the pan with the water. Bring to the boil, reduce the heat and cover the pan. Simmer for 1 hour and allow to cool, then strain the mixture overnight through a jelly bag suspended over a large bowl.

2 The next day, measure the resulting juice and pour it into a large pan. Add 375 g (12 oz) sugar for each 600 ml (1 pint) of juice. Pour in the port and lemon juice and cook over a low heat, stirring continuously, until the sugar has completely dissolved. Increase the heat and bring to the boil, then boil hard to setting point. Using a slotted spoon, carefully skim off any scum.

3 Transfer the jelly to warm dry jars. Cover the surface of each with a disc of waxed paper, waxed side down, then top with an airtight lid or cellophane cover. Label and leave to cool, then store in a cool, dark place. It will keep for 3–4 months.

Sweet Earl Grey and lemon jelly

Delicately flavoured with Earl Grey tea leaves, this elegant jelly is delightful served on thick buttered toast for breakfast, or with scones and whipped cream for afternoon tea.

MAKES: 1.4 kg (2¾ lb)

PREPARATION TIME: 40 minutes, plus straining

COOKING TIME: 55–60 minutes

2 kg (4 lb) cooking apples, cut into 2.5 cm
(1 inch) pieces

1.2 litres (2 pints) water

4 tablespoons Earl Grey tea leaves

1–1.25 kg (2–2½ lb) granulated sugar

juice of 1 lemon

1 Put the apples into a large pan and pour over the water to just cover them. Cover the pan and bring to the boil, then reduce the heat and simmer, still covered, for 45 minutes until the apples are soft.

2 Put a piece of muslin in a bowl, cover with boiling water and leave to stand for 5 minutes. Drain the muslin and lay it flat on a plate. Spoon the tea leaves into the centre, then tie with string and put into a large bowl. Suspend a jelly bag over the bowl, then tip the apples and their cooking liquid into the bag and strain for 4 hours, or overnight. Remove the muslin-tied tea bag after 20–30 minutes, depending on how strong you like your tea.

3 Measure the apple juice and tea-flavoured liquid and pour them into a clean pan. Add 500 g (1 lb) sugar for every 600 ml (1 pint) of liquid. Add the lemon juice and cook over a low heat, stirring continuously, until the sugar has completely dissolved.

4 Increase the heat and bring the jelly to the boil, then boil rapidly for 10–15 minutes, testing at 5-minute intervals until a set is reached. Using a slotted spoon, carefully skim off any scum.

5 Transfer the jelly to warm dry jars. Cover the surface of each with a disc of waxed paper, waxed side down, then top with an airtight lid or cellophane cover. Label and leave to cool, then store in a cool, dark place. It will keep for 6–12 months.

Variation

Add a slice of lemon to each warm jar before pouring in the hot jelly.

Tip

• This preserve comes quickly up to setting point. Don't overheat it or the finished jelly will be spoilt with unsightly threads of overcooked sugar.

Mint and apple jelly
This is a traditional way of preserving mint for use in the very early spring and winter months. You can also try using rosemary instead of mint, or a selection of mixed herbs. Serve with roast lamb.

MAKES: about 1.5–2 kg (3–4 lb)

PREPARATION TIME: 30 minutes, plus straining and standing

COOKING TIME: 1½ hours

2 kg (4 lb) cooking apples, roughly chopped
300 ml (½ pint) white vinegar
600 ml (1 pint) water
1.5 kg (3 lb) sugar
125 g (4 oz) stalks of fresh mint

1 Put the apples into a pan with the vinegar and water. Bring to the boil, then lower the heat and cover the pan. Simmer for 1 hour until the fruit is reduced to a pulp. Allow to cool slightly, then strain the mixture overnight through a jelly bag suspended over a large bowl.

2 The next day, pour the resulting juice into into a large pan and add the sugar. Cook over a low heat, stirring continuously, until the sugar has completely dissolved. Increase the heat and bring to a rapid boil, then boil hard to setting point.

3 Pick the leaves from the mint and chop them finely. Using a slotted spoon, carefully skim off any scum from the jelly, then stir in the mint. Leave to stand for 10 minutes, then stir well and transfer to warm dry jars.

4 Cover the surface of each with a disc of waxed paper, waxed side down, then leave until cold. Top the cold jars with airtight lids or cellophane covers. Label and store in a cool, dark place. It will keep for 3–4 months.

Fruit butters, cheeses and fruit curds

are made from fruit pulp and boiled until they are much thicker than ordinary jam. In fact, fruit cheeses are so thick that when they are ready you should be able to draw a spoon through the mixture and see the bottom of the pan. When cold, they can be cut with a knife and eaten in slices. Butters, by their name, have a softer, more spreadable texture. Both fruit butters and fruit cheeses are best eaten with cold meats or cheese, in place of chutney.

Fruit curds have a natural sharpness and are made not with curd cheese as the name would imply, but with citrus fruit rinds and juice, butter, sugar and eggs, which are cooked in a bowl over a pan of simmering water rather than in direct contact with the heat. Since they contain eggs, their storage life is much shorter than many other preserves.

Banana butter

This preserve is a great favourite with children and is delicious in a simple trifle. Make it when bananas are cheap in local markets or when they are being sold off as slightly over-ripe.

MAKES: about 1 kg (2 lb)
PREPARATION TIME: 10 minutes
COOKING TIME: 1 hour 20 minutes

10 bananas, peeled
juice of 2 lemons
150 ml (¼ pint) water
500 g (1 lb) sugar
¼ teaspoon ground mixed spice

1 Slice the bananas into a large pan and add the lemon juice and water. Bring to the boil, then reduce the heat and cover the pan. Simmer for 20–30 minutes or until the fruit is reduced to a pulp.

2 Press the pulp through a fine sieve into a clean pan. Gradually stir in the sugar over a low heat, then mix in the spice and continue stirring until the sugar has completely dissolved. Increase the heat and bring to the boil, then lower the heat and simmer the butter steadily, uncovered, for 30–40 minutes, stirring frequently, until reduced by half and quite thick.

3 Transfer the butter to warm pots and cover each with a disc of waxed paper, waxed side down, then top with an airtight lid or cellophane cover. Label and leave to cool, then store in a cool dark place for up to 3 months.

Lemon and pear butter

This fruit butter is delicious spread thinly on slices of fresh bread and topped with a little clotted cream. Or use as you would a jam, only perhaps a little more sparingly.

MAKES: about 1 kg (2 lb)
PREPARATION TIME: 25 minutes
COOKING TIME: 2 hours

1 kg (2 lb) pears, roughly chopped
300 ml (½ pint) water
2 lemons, halved
about 750 g (1½ lb) sugar

1 Put the pears into a large pan and add the water. Squeeze the juice from the lemons and pour it into the pan, then chop the lemon shells and stir them in too. Bring to the boil, the reduce the heat and cover the pan. Simmer for about 1 hour or until the fruit is reduced to a pulp.

2 Press the pulp through a fine sieve and weigh the resulting purée, then pour it into a clean pan. Add 375 g (12 oz) sugar for each 500 g (1 lb) of purée and stir over a low heat until the sugar has completely dissolved. Increase the heat and bring to the boil, then lower the heat and simmer steadily, uncovered, for about 45 minutes, stirring frequently, until the butter has thickened to a creamy consistency.

3 Transfer the butter to warm pots and cover each with a disc of waxed paper, waxed side down, then top with an airtight lid or cellophane cover. Label and leave to cool, then store in a cool dark place for up to 3 months.

Spiced apple butter

Windfall apples are ideal for this preserve. Cut out any bad parts before weighing, but do not bother to peel them as the cooked fruit will be sieved.

MAKES: about 1.5 kg (3 lb)

PREPARATION TIME: 20 minutes

COOKING TIME: 1¾ hours

1.25 kg (2½ lb) cooking apples, roughly chopped

1 cinnamon stick

1 teaspoon freshly grated nutmeg

1 lemon, chopped

600 ml (1 pint) water

about 625 g (1¼ lb) sugar

1 Put the apples into a pan with the spices, chopped lemon and the water. Bring to the boil, then reduce the heat and cover the pan. Simmer for 1 hour, or until the fruit is reduced to a pulp.

2 Press the mixture through a fine sieve, then weigh the resulting purée and put it into a clean pan. Add 375 g (12 oz) sugar for each 500 g (1 lb) of purée and cook over a low heat, stirring continuously, until the sugar has completely dissolved. Increase the heat and bring to the boil, then boil hard for about 30 minutes, stirring frequently, until the mixture is reduced by half and is thick and creamy.

3 Transfer the butter to warm pots and cover each with a disc of waxed paper, waxed side down, then top with an airtight lid or cellophane cover. Label and leave to cool, then store in a cool dark place for up to 3 months.

Lime and passion fruit curd

The passion fruit seeds add a wonderful perfume and delicate flavour that's very moreish when spread on warm scones or folded into whipped cream for a wonderfully easy cake filling.

MAKES: 650 g (1 lb 5 oz)
PREPARATION TIME: 15 minutes
COOKING TIME: 30 minutes

250 g (8 oz) caster sugar
juice and grated rind of 4 limes
125 g (4 oz) unsalted butter, cut into pieces
4 eggs
3 passion fruit

1 Quarter fill a medium pan with water and bring to the boil. Set a large bowl on the pan, making sure that the base is not touching the water. Put the sugar and lime rind into the bowl and press against the edge of the bowl with a wooden spoon to release the oils from the rind.

2 Pour the lime juice into the bowl through a sieve and add the butter. Heat, stirring occasionally, until the butter has melted.

3 Beat the eggs in a separate bowl, then strain into the sugar mixture and stir well. Continue cooking for 20–30 minutes, stirring occasionally, until very thick.

4 Take the bowl off the pan. Halve the passion fruit and, using a teaspoon, scoop the seeds into the lime curd. Mix together gently, then transfer to warm dry jars. Cover each with a disc of waxed paper, waxed side down, then top with an airtight lid or cellophane cover. Label and leave to cool, then store in the refrigerator. It will keep for up to 1 month.

Variations

For lemon curd, use 2½ lemons in place of the limes. For a mixed citrus curd use 1 lemon, 1 orange and 1 lime.

Quince cheese
Quinces are intensely fragrant and when cut they have a pale creamy flesh that turns to a delicate pale pink when cooked. Scoop straight out of the jar, or leave to set, slice and serve with strong English cheeses.

MAKES: 1.25 kg (2½ lb)

PREPARATION TIME: 45 minutes

COOKING TIME: 1¾ hours

2 kg (4 lb) quinces
2 litres (3½ pints) water
1.5–1.75 kg (3–3½ lb) preserving sugar
a little sunflower oil or glycerine

1 Rub off any fuzzy down from the quinces, then rinse and drain. Cut the whole fruit into 2.5 cm (1 inch) cubes, put into a large pan and pour the water over so that the fruit is just covered. Cover the pan and bring to the boil, then reduce the heat and simmer for 1 hour until the quinces are very soft.

2 Purée the quinces and their cooking liquid in batches in a food processor or blender, then press through a sieve into a large bowl. Discard the seeds, skins and cores.

3 Weigh the sieved purée and for every 500 g (1 lb) of purée weigh out 500 g (1 lb) of sugar. Pour the sugar into a roasting tin and warm in a low oven (see page 9) for 10 minutes.

4 Wash and dry the pan and brush with a little sunflower oil or glycerine. Pour the puréed quinces back into the pan and heat gently. Stir in the warmed sugar and cook over a low heat, stirring continously, until the sugar has completely dissolved.

5 Increase the heat slightly and cook, uncovered, over a moderate heat for 30–45 minutes, carefully skimming off any scum as needed with a slotted spoon. Stir more frequently towards the end of cooking so that the thickening purée does not stick and burn on the bottom of the pan. When the cheese is almost ready you will find that the mixture will make much larger bubbles and the colour will darken slightly to a rich russet pink. Test for a set. If using a sugar thermometer, it will set at 100°C (212°F), a little lower than the usual jam temperature.

6 This preserve sets fast, so quickly transfer it to warm dry jars, cover each with a disc of waxed paper, waxed side down, then top with an airtight lid or cellophane cover. Label and leave to cool, then store in a cool, dark place. It will keep for 6–12 months.

Cranberry and apple cheese
Fruit cheeses can be sliced and eaten with coffee after a meal and they also make an excellent companion to dairy cheeses.

MAKE: 2 kg (4 lb)

PREPARATION TIME: 20 minutes

COOKING TIME: 1½ hours

1 kg (2 lb) cranberries, defrosted, if frozen

1 kg (2 lb) cooking apples, chopped

75 g (3 oz) orange rind

175 ml (6 fl oz) orange juice

1 teaspoon cloves

1 cinnamon stick

2 mace blades

600 ml (1 pint) water

about 1 kg (2 lb) sugar

vegetable oil, for oiling

1 Put the cranberries, apples, orange rind, orange juice and spices into a large pan. Pour over the water and cover. Bring to the boil, then reduce the heat and simmer, still covered, for about 30 minutes, or until the fruit is soft and pulpy.

2 Press the pulp through a fine sieve and weigh the resulting purée, then pour it into a clean pan. Add 250 g (8 oz) of sugar for each 500 g (1 lb) of purée and cook over a low heat, stirring continuously, until the sugar has completely dissolved. Continue to cook, still stirring, until the purée is very thick. To test if cooked, draw a spoon across the bottom of the pan – it should leave a clean firm line through the mixture.

3 Transfer the cheese immediately to hot oiled pots or moulds and cover each with a disc of waxed paper, waxed side down, and an airtight lid or cellophane cover. Label and leave to cool, then store in a cool, dark place for 1 month, or 3 months in the refrigerator.

Marmalades and mincemeats *Marmalade must by definition be made with citrus fruits, either one type of fruit or a mixture, and is primarily made with bittersweet Seville oranges. Lemons, limes and grapefruits also make excellent marmalade, alone or in combination, while sweet oranges and tangerines are best mixed with sharper lemons, not only to improve flavour, but also to boost setting qualities. Recipes range from clear delicate jelly marmalades speckled with thin shreds of fruit rind, to darker chunkier versions with larger shreds.*

Mincemeat is made with a subtle blend of ground spices, minced or chopped dried fruits, coarsely grated or cooked apples, and sugar and steeped in brandy or whisky. Making mincemeat involves no real cooking (although some recipes do use lightly stewed fresh fruits rather than the traditionally grated), so it is ideal for the novice cook.

Dark orange and lemon marmalade *A small amount of muscovado sugar gives this marmalade a good, rich flavour. For a tangy marmalade, use Seville oranges when they are in season.*

MAKES: about 2 kg (4 lb)

PREPARATION TIME: 30 minutes, plus standing

COOKING TIME: 2 hours

2 large oranges, finely chopped and pips discarded

4 large lemons, finely chopped and pips discarded

1.8 litres (3 pints) water

1 kg (2 lb) sugar

250 g (8 oz) muscovado sugar

1 Put the fruit into a large pan and add the water. Bring to the boil, reduce the heat and cover the pan. Simmer for 1½ hours.

2 Add all the sugar to the pan and cook over a low heat, stirring continuously, until the sugar has completely dissolved. Increase the heat and bring to a rolling boil, then boil hard to setting point. Using a slotted spoon, carefully skim off any scum, then leave the marmalade to stand for 15 minutes to allow the fruit to settle.

3 Stir the marmalade, then transfer to warm dry jars. Cover the surface of each with a disc of waxed paper, waxed side down, then leave until cold. Top the cold jars with airtight lids or cellophane covers. Label and store in a cool, dark place. It will keep for 3–4 months.

Dark orange and lemon marmalade

Seville orange marmalade

Seville oranges are only obtainable for a short time in January. They are extremely bitter and make the best marmalade.

MAKES: about 3.25 kg (7 lb)
PREPARATION TIME: 45 minutes, plus standing
COOKING TIME: 2¾ hours

1 kg (2 lb) Seville oranges
2.5 litres (4 pints) water
2 kg (4 lb) sugar
juice of 3 lemons

1 Thinly peel the rind from the oranges and cut it into fine shreds. Halve the fruit and squeeze out the juice, then put the orange juice and rind into a large pan with the water. Chop the orange halves, including the pith, and tie the pieces in a muslin bag. Add this to the pan and bring the mixture slowly to the boil. Reduce the heat, cover the pan and simmer for 2 hours.

2 Take the pan off the heat and leave to stand until the muslin is cool enough to handle, then squeeze all the juices back into the pan and discard the bag.

3 Add the sugar and lemon juice and cook over a low heat, stirring continuously, until the sugar has completely dissolved. Increase the heat and bring to the boil, then boil hard to setting point. Using a slotted spoon, carefully skim off any scum, then leave the marmalade to stand for 15 minutes to allow the fruit to settle.

4 Stir well, then transfer to warm dry jars. Cover the surface of each with a disc of waxed paper, waxed side down, then leave until cold. Top the cold jars with airtight lids or cellophane covers. Label and store in a cool, dark place. It will keep for 3–4 months.

Three-fruit processor marmalade

If you would like to make marmalade, but are a little short of time, then this speedy fine-shred version uses a food processor to cut down on preparation time.

MAKES: 2.25 kg (5 lb)

PREPARATION TIME: 30 minutes, plus straining and standing

COOKING TIME: about 1¼ hours

4 oranges

3 limes

2 lemons

1.5 litres (2½ pints) water

1.5 kg (3 lb) preserving or granulated sugar

1 Thinly peel the rinds from the fruit, leaving the white pith behind. Put the rinds into a food processor and chop finely, then tip out on to a plate and reserve.

2 Quarter the fruits and process in two batches until roughly chopped, then put them into a large pan with the water. Cover the pan and bring to the boil, then reduce the heat and simmer for 45 minutes until the pith is soft.

3 Pour the mixture through a fine sieve into a bowl and leave to drip for 30 minutes. Press out any remaining juice from the pith with the back of a spoon, then pour the juice back into the pan and add the chopped fruit rinds. Cover and simmer gently for 15 minutes until tender. Meanwhile, pour the sugar into a roasting tin and warm in a low oven (see page 9) for 10 minutes.

4 Add the warmed sugar to the pan and cook over a low heat, stirring continuously, until the sugar has completely dissolved. Increase the heat, bring to the boil and boil, uncovered, for 10–15 minutes, testing at 5-minute intervals until a set is reached. Using a slotted spoon, carefully skim off any scum, then leave the marmalade to stand for 15 minutes to allow the fruit to settle.

5 Stir well, then transfer to warm dry jars. Cover the surface of each with a disc of waxed paper, waxed side down, then leave until cold. Top the cold jars with airtight lids or cellophane covers. Label and store in a cool, dark place. It will keep for 6–12 months.

Ginger marmalade

Home-made marmalade is always much nicer than the shop-bought variety and nowhere is this more true than with the slightly unusual preserves. For extra zing, just add more ginger.

MAKES: about 2.25 kg (5 lb)

PREPARATION TIME: 30 minutes, plus standing

COOKING TIME: 2¾ hours

8 lemons

2 large oranges

2.5 litres (4 pints) water

125 g (4 oz) fresh root ginger, thinly peeled, sliced and finely shredded

1.5 kg (3 lb) sugar

1 Thinly peel the rinds from the fruit and cut them into fine shreds. Halve the fruit and squeeze out the juice, then put the juice and rinds into a large pan with the water and ginger.

2 Chop the lemon and orange halves, including the pith, and tie the pieces in a muslin bag. Add this to the pan and slowly bring the mixture to the boil. Reduce the heat, cover the pan and simmer for 2 hours or until the ginger and fruit rinds are completely tender. Take the pan off the heat and leave to stand until the muslin is cool enough to handle, then squeeze all the juices back into the marmalade and discard the bag.

3 Add the sugar to the pan and cook over a low heat, stirring continuously, until the sugar has completely dissolved. Increase the heat and bring to the boil, then boil hard to setting point. Using a slotted spoon, carefully skim off any scum, then leave the marmalade to stand for 15 minutes to allow the fruit to settle.

4 Stir well, then transfer to warm dry jars. Cover the surface of each with a disc of waxed paper, waxed side down, then leave until cold. Top the cold jars with airtight lids or cellophane covers. Label and store in a cool, dark place. It will keep for 3–4 months.

Lime marmalade
This is a delicious, flavoursome and slightly tangy marmalade. Although limes are sometimes quite expensive, this recipe gives a high yield, which compensates for the initial cost of the fruit.

MAKES: about 2.25 kg (5 lb)

PREPARATION TIME: 30 minutes, plus standing

COOKING TIME: 2¼ hours

6 limes, washed, dried and quartered lengthways

2 lemons, washed, dried and quartered lengthways

1.5 litres (2½ pints) water

1.5 kg (3 lb) sugar

1 Cut the lime quarters into long, very fine slices, removing all the pips. Cut the lemon quarters in the same way and mix both fruits in a large pan. Pour in the water and bring to the boil, then reduce the heat and cover the pan. Simmer for 1½ hours.

2 Add the sugar to the pan and cook over a low heat, stirring continuously, until the sugar has completely dissolved. Increase the heat and bring to the boil, then boil hard to setting point. Using a slotted spoon, carefully skim off any scum, then leave the marmalade to stand for 15 minutes to allow the fruit to settle.

3 Stir well, then transfer to warm dry jars. Cover the surface of each with a disc of waxed paper, waxed side down, then leave until cold. Top the cold jars with airtight lids or cellophane covers. Label and store in a cool, dark place. It will keep for 3–4 months.

Spiced cranberry mincemeat with port *This*

chunky, luxury mincemeat captures all the very best Christmas aromas in a jar. Spoon into pastry cases for truly memorable mince pies and tarts.

MAKES: 1.6 kg (3¼ lb)

PREPARATION TIME: 20 minutes, plus standing

COOKING TIME: 5 minutes

250 g (8 oz) cranberries

1 large cooking apple, about 375 g (12 oz), peeled, cored and diced

500 g (1 lb) bag luxury mixed dried fruit

1 teaspoon ground cinnamon

½ teaspoon freshly grated nutmeg

¼ teaspoon ground cloves

200 g (7 oz) soft light brown sugar

125 g (4 oz) vegetable suet

grated rind of 1 orange

125 ml (4 fl oz) ruby port

1 Put the cranberries and apple into a pan with 3 tablespoons of water and cook, uncovered, for 5 minutes, stirring occasionally, until the fruits are softened but still holding their shape. Leave to cool in the pan.

2 Put the dried fruit into a large bowl and mix in the remaining ingredients. Stir in the cooled cooked fruit, then cover the bowl and leave to stand overnight.

3 Stir the mincemeat mixture again, then spoon into warm dry jars. Cover the surface of each with a disc of waxed paper, waxed side down, then top with an airtight lid. Label and leave to mature in a cool, dark place for 3-4 weeks before using, or store, unopened, for up to 6 months.

Tip
• If you prefer a more traditional 'minced meat' texture either put the dried fruits through a mincer or chop them in a food processor.

Spiced cranberry mincemeat with port

Apricot and ginger mincemeat

Dried apricots and crystallized ginger make a deliciously unusual mincemeat. Try this recipe as an alternative to traditional mincemeat when making mince pies for Christmas.

MAKES: about 2 kg (4 lb)

PREPARATION TIME: 30 minutes, plus standing

50 g (2 oz) crystallized ginger, finely chopped

250 g (8 oz) dried apricots, finely chopped

250 g (8 oz) raisins, finely chopped

175 g (6 oz) sultanas, finely chopped

175 g (6 oz) currants

50 g (2 oz) chopped mixed peel

50 g (2 oz) blanched almonds, chopped

250 g (8 oz) cooking apples, peeled, cored and grated

juice and grated rind of 3 oranges

juice and grated rind of 2 lemons

250 g (8 oz) soft light brown sugar

375 g (12 oz) carrots, peeled and grated

¼ teaspoon freshly grated nutmeg

½ teaspoon ground mixed spice

150 ml (¼ pint) brandy

4 tablespoons rum

1 Put the ginger, apricots, raisins and sultanas into a large bowl with the currants, mixed peel and almonds.

2 Put the apples into a separate bowl and mix in the orange and lemon rinds and juices, then stir into the chopped fruit with the sugar.

3 Next, add the carrots to the bowl with the spices, brandy and rum, then cover the bowl and leave the mincemeat to stand for 2 days, stirring it frequently.

4 Transfer the mincemeat to clean dry jars and cover the surface of each with a disc of waxed paper, waxed side down, then top with an airtight lid. Label and leave to mature in a cool, dark place for 3–4 weeks before using, or store, unopened, for up to 6 months.

Traditional mincemeat

At one time mincemeat comprised minced meat and dried fruit, but over the years it has become a mixture of suet, dried fruits, apples and brandy or rum.

MAKES: about 2 kg (4 lb)

PREPARATION TIME: 30 minutes, plus standing

250 g (8 oz) raisins, minced or finely chopped

250 g (8 oz) sultanas, minced or finely chopped

250 g (8 oz) currants, minced or finely chopped

250 g (8 oz) shredded suet

125 g (4 oz) chopped mixed peel

125 g (4 oz) blanched almonds, chopped

500 g (1 lb) cooking apples, peeled, cored and grated

1 large carrot, peeled and grated

juice and grated rind of 1 orange

juice of 2 lemons

250 g (8 oz) soft dark brown sugar

½ teaspoon freshly grated nutmeg

½ teaspoon ground cinnamon

150 ml (¼ pint) brandy or rum

4 tablespoons dry sherry

1 Mix the raisins, sultanas and currants with the suet and mixed peel in a large bowl. Stir in the almonds, apples, carrot, orange juice and rind, lemon juice and sugar, then stir in the spices and pour over the brandy or rum and the sherry.

2 Mix thoroughly to combine all the ingredients, then cover the bowl and leave the mincemeat to stand for 2 days, stirring it frequently.

3 Transfer the mincemeat to clean dry jars and cover the surface of each with a disc of waxed paper, waxed side down, then top with an airtight lid. Label and leave to mature in a cool, dark place for 3–4 weeks before using, or store, unopened, for up to 6 months.

Variation

For an economical mincemeat, use 150 ml (¼ pint) sherry and just 4 tablespoons of brandy or rum instead of vice versa.

Chutneys and pickles *As you don't need to worry about testing for a set, these delicious sweet and sour savoury preserves are an ideal starting point for the beginner. When making chutney or cooked relishes, simply finely shred or dice a mix of fruit and vegetables, then put them into a large pan with sugar, vinegar and flavourings and simmer gently until thick. Flavourings can be as exotic or simple as you like. Choose from Thai-inspired blends of lime leaves, galangal, ginger and lemon grass, Indian spice mixes with turmeric, paprika, cardamom, ginger, cumin and coriander, or Mediterranean mixes of garlic and herbs, juniper, allspice and cinnamon.*

Pickles tend to be made with larger pieces or whole fruits or vegetables steeped in a flavoured and sweetened vinegar and, unlike chutneys, the fruit and vegetables are preserved while still raw.

Green tomato chutney

If you grow tomatoes you will probably be left with some unripened fruit at the end of the season. But don't throw your green tomatoes away: chop them up and make a tempting chutney.

MAKES: about 2 kg (4 lb)

PREPARATION TIME: 15 minutes

COOKING TIME: 1 hour 40 minutes

1 kg (2 lb) green tomatoes, finely chopped

500 g (1 lb) onions, finely chopped

500 g (1 lb) cooking apples, peeled, cored and chopped

2 fresh green chillies, halved, deseeded and finely chopped

2 garlic cloves, crushed

1 teaspoon ground ginger

generous pinch of ground cloves

generous pinch of ground turmeric

50 g (2 oz) raisins

250 g (8 oz) soft dark brown sugar

300 ml (½ pint) white wine vinegar

1 Put the tomatoes, onions, apples and chillies into a large pan and mix together. Add the garlic, ginger, cloves and turmeric, then stir in the raisins, sugar and vinegar.

2 Bring to the boil, reduce the heat and cover the pan. Simmer, stirring frequently, for 1¼–1½ hours or until the chutney has thickened.

3 Transfer the chutney to warm dry jars and cover the surface of each with a disc of waxed paper, waxed side down, then top with an airtight lid. Label and leave to mature in a cool, dark place for at least 3 weeks before using, or store, unopened, for 6–12 months.

Green tomato chutney

Red onion and raisin chutney

This tasty preserve is quick and easy to prepare and cook. Serve on toast topped with grilled Cheddar or goats' cheese or spice up a simple ham or cold turkey sandwich.

MAKES: 1.4 kg (2¾ lb)

PREPARATION TIME: 15 minutes

COOKING TIME: 35–40 minutes

3 tablespoons virgin olive oil

1.5 kg (3 lb) red onions, halved and thinly sliced

250 g (8 oz) soft light brown sugar

300 ml (½ pint) red wine vinegar

200 g (7 oz) raisins

3 garlic cloves, finely chopped

3 bay leaves

1 tablespoon wholegrain mustard

½ teaspoon pimenton (smoked hot paprika)

½ teaspoon salt

freshly ground black pepper

1 Heat the oil in a large pan, add the onions and cook gently for 10 minutes until softened but not browned.

2 Stir in 3 tablespoons of the sugar and fry gently for 15 minutes, stirring until just beginning to brown.

3 Add the rest of the sugar and the other remaining ingredients, mix well and simmer, uncovered, for 10–15 minutes, stirring occasionally, until the onions are soft and the liquid has reduced and thickened.

4 Transfer the chutney to warm dry jars. Cover the surface of each with a disc of waxed paper, waxed side down, then top with an airtight lid. Label and leave to cool in a cool, dark place. It will keep for 6–12 months.

Variation

For a Christmas version, add half raisins and half cranberries or all cranberries and extra sugar.

Peach and date chutney

The delicate flavour of the peaches makes this a good accompaniment to ripe, creamy Brie, full-fat soft cheeses and roast poultry. Perfect for serving with your cold roast Christmas turkey.

MAKES: 1.5–2 kg (3–4 lb)

PREPARATION TIME: 10 minutes

COOKING TIME: 50 minutes

12 peaches

500 g (1 lb) onions

2 garlic cloves, crushed

2 tablespoons grated fresh root ginger

125 g (4 oz) pitted dates, chopped

250 g (8 oz) demerara sugar

300 ml (½ pint) red wine vinegar

salt and freshly ground black pepper

1 Put the peaches into a large bowl, cover them with boiling water and leave to stand for about 1 minute, then drain and peel them. Halve and stone the fruit and cut it into thick slices.

2 Put the onions into a pan with the peaches, garlic, ginger, dates, sugar and vinegar. Add a generous sprinkling of salt and pepper and bring the mixture to the boil, stirring continuously, until the sugar has completely dissolved.

3 Reduce the heat, cover the pan and simmer, stirring frequently, for 45 minutes, until the chutney has thickened.

4 Transfer the chutney to warm dry jars. Cover the surface of each with a disc of waxed paper, waxed side down, then top with an airtight lid. Label and leave to mature in a cool, dark place for 2 weeks before using, or store, unopened, for 6–12 months.

Chestnut, red onion and fennel chutney *This chutney is quick and easy to prepare and is the perfect partner to blue cheese, bread and cold meats for a quick and delicious lunch.*

MAKES: about 625 g (1¼ lb)

PREPARATION TIME: 15 minutes

COOKING TIME: 1½ hours

60 ml (2½ fl oz) olive oil

4 large red onions, thinly sliced

1 fennel bulb, trimmed and thinly sliced

250 g (8 oz) cooked, peeled chestnuts, halved

100 g (3½ oz) soft light brown sugar

125 ml (4 fl oz) cider vinegar

125 ml (4 fl oz) sweet sherry or marsala wine

freshly ground black pepper

1 Heat the oil in a large pan, add the onions and fennel and cook gently for 25–30 minutes, until the onions are very soft.

2 Add the chestnuts, sugar, vinegar and sherry to the pan, season well with pepper and stir. Simmer gently, uncovered, stirring occasionally, for about 1 hour, until the chutney has thickened.

3 Transfer the chutney to a warm dry jar and cover the surface with a disc of waxed paper, waxed side down, then top with an airtight lid. Label and leave to cool completely before serving. Store in a cool, dark place or in the refrigerator. It will keep for 3–4 months.

Chestnut, red onion and fennel chutney

Tamarind and date chutney
This sweet and sour relish makes a great accompaniment to Indian food, but is also wonderful in a cheese sandwich.

MAKES: about 200 g (7 oz)

PREPARATION TIME: 10 minutes

200 g (7 oz) pitted dried dates, roughly
   chopped

1 tablespoon tamarind paste

1 teaspoon ground cumin

1 teaspoon chilli powder

1 tablespoon tomato ketchup

200 ml (7 fl oz) water

sea salt

1 Put all the ingredients into a food processor or blender and process until fairly smooth.

2 Transfer the chutney to a serving bowl, cover and chill until required. It will keep for up to 3 days in the refrigerator.

Mango, apple and mint chutney
This relish would make a tasty accompaniment to any meal, but is particularly delicious with spicy fish cakes.

MAKES: about 200 g (7 oz)

PREPARATION TIME: 10 minutes

1 raw green mango, peeled, stoned and
   roughly chopped

1 small apple, peeled, cored and roughly
   chopped

1 teaspoon sea salt

1 tablespoon chopped mint leaves

1 teaspoon mild chilli powder

1 teaspoon soft light brown sugar

150 ml (¼ pint) water

1 Put all the ingredients into a food processor or blender and process until smooth.

2 Transfer the chutney to a small serving dish, cover and chill until required.

Chilli and garlic chutney

Be warned – this spicy chutney is very hot. Serve with curries or mix a little with natural yogurt and spread the mixture over meat or poultry before cooking to make an exciting marinade.

MAKES: 750 g–1 kg (1½–2 lb)

PREPARATION TIME: 15 minutes

COOKING TIME: 30 minutes

500 g (1 lb) fresh chillies, red or green

6 garlic cloves, crushed

4 tablespoons ground cumin

2 tablespoons ground turmeric

1 large onion, finely chopped

1 tablespoon salt

25 g (1 oz) fresh root ginger, grated

300 ml (½ pint) groundnut oil

3 tablespoons muscovado sugar

300 ml (½ pint) white wine vinegar

1 Remove the stalks from the chillies then chop the chillies very finely, seeds and all.

2 Mix the chillies, garlic, cumin, turmeric, onion, salt, ginger and oil in a pan and fry for 15 minutes, stirring frequently. Add the sugar and vinegar and bring the mixture to the boil, then cover the pan and boil the chutney for 10 minutes, stirring occasionally.

3 Transfer the chutney to hot dry jars and cover the surface of each with a disc of waxed paper, waxed side down, then top with an airtight lid. Label and leave to cool completely before serving. Store in a cool, dark place or in the refrigerator. It will keep for up to 12 months. Stir the chutney well before using as the oil will separate out on standing.

Piccalilli
This pickle is traditionally very spicy with a crunchy texture. It is usually served with cold meats such as ham or roast pork, but can also do a wonderful job of spicing up a cheese sandwich.

MAKES: about 1 kg (2 lb)

PREPARATION TIME: 10 minutes, plus standing

COOKING TIME: 25 minutes

1 small cauliflower, broken into small florets, large stalks discarded

½ cucumber, thinly peeled and roughly chopped

2 onions, chopped

2 large carrots, peeled and cut into chunks

about 50 g (2 oz) salt

2 tablespoons plain flour

300 ml (½ pint) cider vinegar

250 g (8 oz) sugar

½ teaspoon ground turmeric

½ teaspoon ground ginger

2 teaspoons mustard powder

freshly ground black pepper

1 Layer the vegetables in a large bowl, sprinkling each layer with salt, then cover and leave to stand overnight. The next day, lightly rinse and thoroughly dry them.

2 Mix the flour to a smooth cream with a little of the vinegar. Heat the remaining vinegar in a large pan with the sugar, spices and mustard over a low heat, stirring continuously, until the sugar has dissolved. Increase the heat and bring to the boil, then season the mixture generously with pepper and add the vegetables. Bring back to the boil, then reduce the heat and simmer, uncovered, for 10 minutes.

3 Remove the pan from the heat and gradually stir in the flour mixture. Return to the heat, bring to the boil and simmer for a further 5 minutes. Transfer the pickle to warm dry jars and top with airtight lids. Label and leave to cool completely before serving. Store in a cool, dark place or in the refrigerator. It will keep for 6–9 months.

Marrow and onion pickle *This is a chunky, sweet pickle, which tastes good with boiled or baked ham, roast meats and continental sausages.*

MAKES: about 2.75 kg (6 lb)

PREPARATION TIME: 30 minutes, plus standing

COOKING TIME: 1¾ hours

1 medium marrow, about 2 kg (4 lb), peeled, halved lengthways and seeded

1 kg (2 lb) small pickling onions, halved

1 green or red pepper

250 g (8 oz) pitted dates

1 tablespoon freshly grated root ginger

600 ml (1 pint) spiced vinegar (see page 105)

500 g (1 lb) demerara sugar

salt

1 Cut the marrow flesh into chunks and layer with the onions in a large bowl, salting each layer, then cover the bowl and leave overnight. The next day, lightly rinse and thoroughly dry the vegetables.

2 Put the salted vegetables into a large pan. Trim and deseed the pepper, remove the pith and chop the flesh finely. Chop the dates finely. Add these ingredients to the pan with the ginger, vinegar and sugar. Bring the mixture to the boil, stirring well to mix the ingredients. Reduce the heat, cover the pan and simmer, stirring frequently, for 1½ hours, until the mixture has thickened.

3 Transfer the pickle to warm dry jars and top with airtight lids. Label and leave to mature in a cool, dark place for 2 weeks before using, or store, unopened, for about 6 months.

Red pepper pickle *The combination of dates and peppers in this pickle makes it the perfect accompaniment to mild cheeses, plain pizzas and simple cold pies.*

MAKES: about 1.5 kg (3 lb)

PREPARATION TIME: 25 minutes

COOKING TIME: about 2 hours

3 large red peppers, halved, cored, deseeded and chopped

500 g (1 lb) cooking apples, peeled, cored and sliced

500 g (1 lb) onions, chopped

250 g (8 oz) pitted dates, chopped

250 g (8 oz) soft dark brown sugar

300 ml (½ pint) red wine vinegar

½ teaspoon salt

1 Mix all the ingredients in a large pan and bring slowly to the boil.

2 Reduce the heat, cover the pan and cook for 1 hour, stirring occasionally, then remove the lid and simmer for about 45 minutes. By this time, most of the excess moisture should have evaporated to leave a thickened pickle.

3 Transfer the pickle to warm dry jars and top with airtight lids. Label and leave to mature in a cool, dark place for 2 weeks before using, or store, unopened, for about 9 months.

Lime pickle
This spicy pickle is served as an accompaniment to many Indian dishes but is also wonderful served just with rice, yogurt and a simple dhal.

MAKES: 500 g (1 lb)

PREPARATION TIME: 10 minutes

COOKING TIME: 5 minutes

10 limes, each cut into 6 sections

125 g (4 oz) sea salt

1 tablespoon fenugreek seeds

1 tablespoon black mustard seeds

1 tablespoon chilli powder

1 tablespoon ground turmeric

300 ml (½ pint) vegetable oil

½ teaspoon ground asafoetida

1 Put the limes into a large jar and cover with the salt.

2 Dry-fry the fenugreek and mustard seeds in a small nonstick frying pan, then grind them to a powder in either a mortar with a pestle, a spice grinder or a coffee grinder kept specially for the purpose.

3 Add the ground seeds, chilli powder and turmeric to the limes and mix well.

4 Heat the oil in a small frying pan until smoking, add the asafoetida and fry for 30 seconds. Pour the oil over the limes and mix well.

5 Cover the jar with a clean cloth and leave to mature for 10 days in a bright, warm place. Top with an airtight lid. Label and store in a cool, dark place. It will keep for 2 months.

Relishes, mustards, sauces and ketchups

These aromatic, spicy condiments pep up even the simplest supper. Unlike chutneys and pickles, they should be served in small quantities, especially mustards, which can vary considerably in strength. White mustard seeds make the mildest mustard, brown seeds a medium strength, while black seeds produce a more fiery condiment. Roughly crushed or finely ground seeds can be flavoured with a wide range of seasonings and sweeteners from chillies, garlic, herbs and horseradish to honey, brown sugar and even red wine or Champagne.

Relishes may be made with raw or cooked vegetables and, like mustard, have a strong flavour. Spices tend to be influenced by Indian and European cuisines, while ketchups and sauces date back to Victorian England. Ketchups require heat treatment or sterilizing to lengthen storage times, unlike condiments that contain vinegar, such as mustards and relishes.

Beetroot and apple relish

Relishes, as their name suggests, are spicy and particularly suitable for serving with grills and barbecues. The beetroot in this recipe gives this relish a wonderful fresh taste.

MAKES: about 1.5 kg (3 lb)

PREPARATION TIME: 15 minutes

COOKING TIME: 1¾ hours

500 g (1 lb) cooking apples, peeled, halved and cored

500 g (1 lb) raw beetroot, peeled

375 g (12 oz) onions, finely chopped

1 tablespoon finely chopped fresh root ginger

2 large garlic cloves, crushed

1 teaspoon paprika

1 teaspoon ground turmeric

1 cinnamon stick

250 g (8 oz) soft dark brown sugar

450 ml (¾ pint) red wine vinegar

1 Grate the apples and beetroot into a large pan, then add all the remaining ingredients.

2 Bring the mixture to the boil, then reduce the heat and cover the pan. Simmer, stirring occasionally, for about 1½ hours, until the relish has thickened and the beetroot is tender.

3 Transfer the relish to warm dry jars and top with airtight lids. Label and leave to mature in a cool, dark place for about 1 week before using, or store, unopened, for 6–9 months.

Beetroot and apple relish

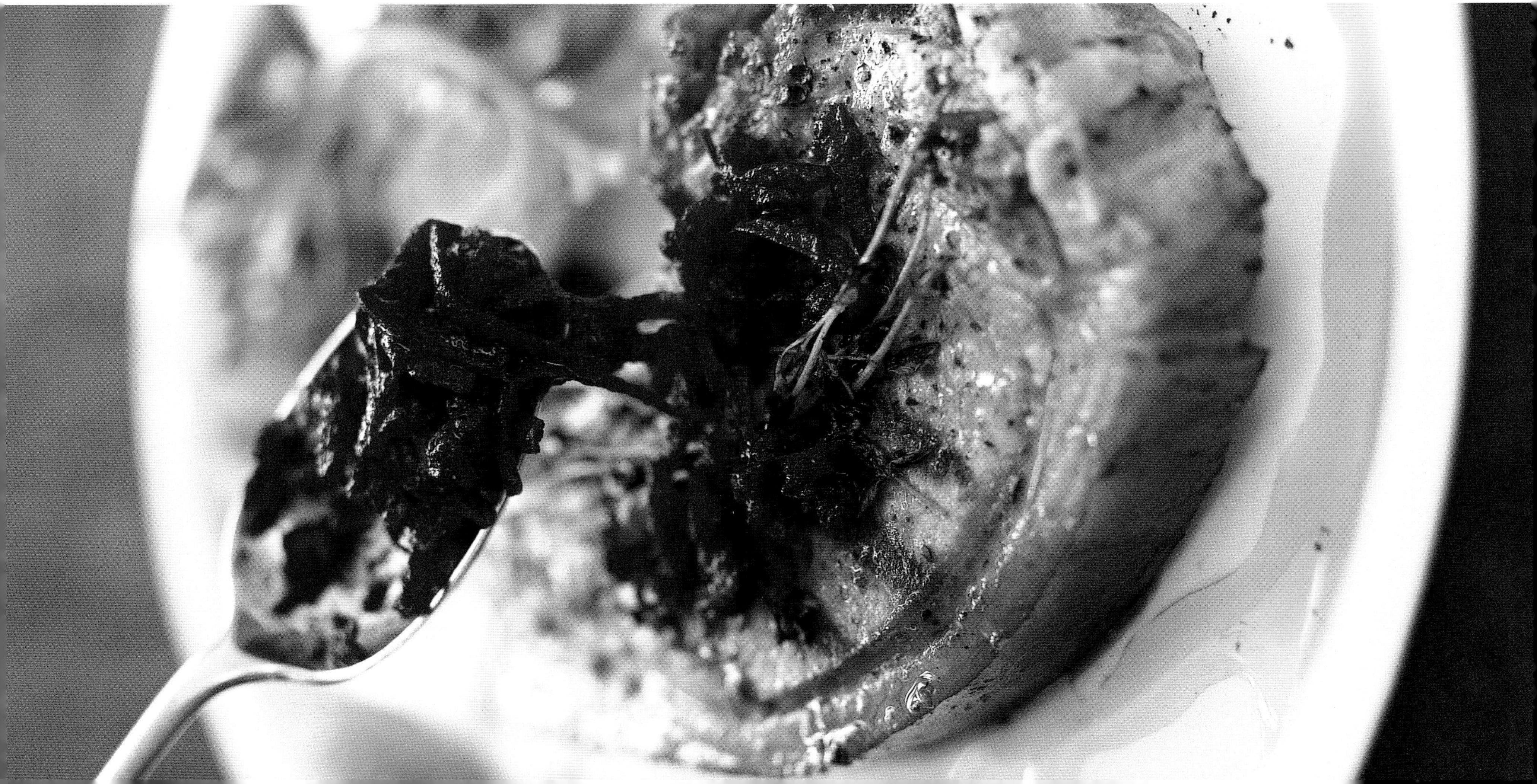

Spiced ginger and coconut relish *This southern Indian relish is a delicious accompaniment to any meal and, despite the many ingredients, is very quick and easy to make.*

MAKES: about 200 g (7 oz)

PREPARATION TIME: 10 minutes

COOKING TIME: 2–3 minutes

2 tablespoons grated fresh root ginger

2 garlic cloves, roughly chopped

1 tablespoon grated fresh coconut or
   2 tablespoons desiccated coconut

2 fresh green chillies, halved and deseeded

1 teaspoon sea salt

1 teaspoon sugar

150 ml (¼ pint) natural yogurt, beaten

2 tablespoons vegetable oil

1 teaspoon black mustard seeds

6–8 curry leaves

1 Put the ginger, garlic, coconut, chillies, salt and sugar into a food processor or blender and process until smooth. Add the yogurt and process for a few seconds, then transfer to a bowl and set aside.

2 Heat the oil in a small nonstick frying pan and, when hot, add the mustard seeds and curry leaves. When the seeds start to pop, remove the pan from the heat, pour the spiced oil over the yogurt mixture and mix well. Keep refrigerated for up to one week.

Cauliflower relish *Cauliflower should never be overcooked as this will completely ruin the texture and taste. This relish is a delicious, crunchy accompaniment to kebabs and samosas.*

MAKES: about 400 g (13 oz)

PREPARATION TIME: 10 minutes

COOKING TIME: 7–8 minutes

2 tablespoons vegetable oil

2 teaspoons black mustard seeds

½ teaspoon ground turmeric

½ teaspoon asafoetida

1 small cauliflower, cut into bite-sized pieces

1 red onion, finely chopped

1 fresh green chilli, halved, deseeded and
   finely chopped

lemon juice

sea salt

1 Heat the oil in a large nonstick frying pan and, when hot, add the mustard seeds, turmeric and asafoetida. When the seeds start to pop, add the cauliflower, onion and chilli. Stir-fry for 5 minutes, then remove from the heat. The cauliflower should have bite to it.

2 Season the relish with lemon juice and salt to taste. Serve at room temperature.

Sweetcorn relish

No selection of pickles and relishes would be complete without American corn relish. Traditionally served with hamburgers, it is also wonderful with pizzas, cottage pie, cold roast meats and cheese.

MAKES: about 1.5 kg (3 lb)

PREPARATION TIME: 15 minutes

COOKING TIME: 30 minutes

4 tablespoons corn oil

2 large onions, finely chopped

1 green pepper, cored, deseeded and finely chopped

1 red pepper, cored, deseeded and finely chopped

4 celery sticks, finely chopped

1 teaspoon salt

1 large garlic clove, crushed

2 carrots, peeled and cut into small cubes

50 g (2 oz) sugar

2 teaspoons mustard powder

750 g (1½ lb) frozen sweetcorn

450 ml (¾ pint) vinegar

1 Heat the oil in a large pan and add the onions, peppers and celery. Fry them until they are soft but not browned, then add the salt and garlic.

2 Add all the remaining ingredients to the pan and bring the mixture to the boil. Reduce the heat and cook, uncovered, for 15 minutes, stirring occasionally.

3 Transfer the relish to warm dry jars, pressing the vegetables well down into the juices, then top with airtight lids and leave to cool.

4 This relish does not need time to mature, but if not immediately consumed, label and store in a cool, dark place for 6 months.

Tomato ketchup

Home-made ketchups are very different from the commercial product. They are spiced fruit or vegetable purées that can be delicate or pronounced in flavour.

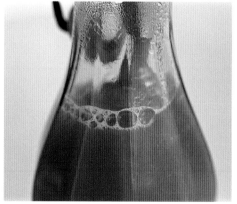

MAKES: about 1.2 litres (2 pints)
PREPARATION TIME: 15 minutes
COOKING TIME: 1 hour

1.5 kg (3 lb) ripe tomatoes (preferably home-grown for a good flavour), roughly chopped
500 g (1 lb) onions, roughly chopped
125 g (4 oz) sugar
3 tablespoons mustard powder
3 garlic cloves, crushed
1 teaspoon salt
150 ml (¼ pint) red wine vinegar

1 Put all the ingredients into a pan and mix well. Bring the mixture to the boil, then reduce the heat and simmer, uncovered, stirring occasionally, for 45 minutes.

2 Allow the ketchup to cool slightly, then blend it to a purée in a food processor or blender. Press the purée through a sieve and return it to the rinsed-out pan.

3 Bring the ketchup back to boiling point, then take the pan off the heat. Transfer the ketchup to warm dry bottles and seal with airtight tops. Label and leave to cool, then store in a cool, dark place. It will keep for up to 6 months.

Mushroom ketchup *This is a simple recipe, which produces a well-flavoured ketchup, useful as a seasoning for casseroles, meat loaves and pies, and dark rich sauces and gravies.*

MAKES: 600 ml (1 pint)

PREPARATION TIME: 10 minutes

COOKING TIME: 45 minutes

375 g (12 oz) large field mushrooms, quartered

300 ml (½ pint) red or white wine vinegar

1 tablespoon salt

125 g (4 oz) soft dark brown sugar

freshly ground black pepper

1 Put all the ingredients into a pan, season generously with pepper and bring the mixture to the boil, stirring frequently to mix in and shrink the mushrooms. Reduce the heat, cover the pan and simmer, stirring occasionally, for 30–40 minutes.

2 Allow the ketchup to cool slightly, then blend it to a purée in a food processor. Return the purée to the rinsed pan and bring it back to boiling point, then take the pan off the heat. Transfer the ketchup to warm dry bottles and seal with airtight tops. Label and store in a cool, dark place. It will keep for up to 6 months.

Spiced orange mustard *This strongly spiced mustard makes the perfect accompaniment to steak and chips, cold roast lamb or turkey, or bubble and squeak.*

MAKES: 425 g (14 oz)

PREPARATION TIME: 15 minutes, plus standing

50 g (2 oz) white mustard seeds

50 g (2 oz) black mustard seeds

75 g (3 oz) soft light brown sugar

2 teaspoons allspice berries

pinch of ground cinnamon

1 teaspoon coarse salt

1 teaspoon peppercorns

1 teaspoon paprika

½ teaspoon ground turmeric

250 ml (8 fl oz) red wine vinegar

grated rind and 3 tablespoons juice of 1 orange

1 Put all the dry ingredients into a food processor or blender and blend until the seeds are roughly crushed.

2 Gradually pour in the vinegar and blend until well mixed. Add the orange rind and juice and blend briefly.

3 Leave the mustard to stand for 1 hour to thicken, then transfer to warm dry jars. Cover the surface of each with a disc of waxed paper, waxed side down, then leave until cold. Top the cold jars with airtight lids. Label and store in a cool, dark place. It will keep for 3–6 months.

Wholegrain mustard with garlic and fennel

Garlicky, with a hint of aniseed, this rustic mustard is perfect served with grilled apple and pork sausages or roasted pork chops.

MAKES: 425 g (14 oz)

PREPARATION TIME: 15 minutes, plus standing

50 g (2 oz) white mustard seeds
50 g (2 oz) black mustard seeds
75 g (3 oz) soft light brown sugar
1 teaspoon fennel seeds
1 teaspoon coarse salt
1 teaspoon peppercorns
½ teaspoon ground turmeric
3 garlic cloves
300 ml (½ pint) cider vinegar

1 Put all the dry ingredients and the garlic into a food processor and blend until the seeds are roughly crushed.

2 Gradually pour in the vinegar and blend until well mixed.

3 Leave the mustard to stand for 1 hour to thicken, then transfer to warm dry jars. Cover the surface of each with a disc of waxed paper, waxed side down, then leave until cold. Top the cold jars with airtight lids or cellophane covers. Label and store in a cool, dark place. It will keep for 3–6 months.

White mustard with fine herbs

Attractively flecked with fresh herbs, this mustard is delicious added to salad dressings. It can also be added to meaty sauces or served on its own with cold meats.

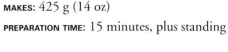

MAKES: 425 g (14 oz)

PREPARATION TIME: 15 minutes, plus standing

100 g (3½ oz) white mustard seeds

75 g (3 oz) soft light brown sugar

1 teaspoon rock salt

1 teaspoon white peppercorns

½ teaspoon ground turmeric

275 ml (9 fl oz) white wine vinegar

6 tablespoons chopped fresh herbs to include rosemary, sage, parsley, chives

1 Put all the dry ingredients into a food processor or blender and blend until the seeds are finely ground.

2 Gradually pour in the vinegar and blend until well mixed. Add the herbs and mix briefly.

3 Leave the mustard to stand for 1 hour to thicken, then transfer to warm dry jars. Cover the surface of each with a disc of waxed paper, waxed side down, then leave until cold. Top the cold jars with airtight lids or cellophane covers. Label and store in a cool, dark place. It will keep for 3–6 months.

Variation

If you would prefer to use just one type of herb, then reduce the total amount to 3 tablespoons.

Cranberry sauce

Although cranberries are too sour to eat raw, they can be transformed through cooking and, with the addition of port or sherry, will produce a delicious sweet, sharp sauce.

MAKES: about 250 g (8 oz)

PREPARATION TIME: 5 minutes

COOKING TIME: 20 minutes

2 tablespoons water

75 g (3 oz) sugar

375 g (12 oz) cranberries

1 tablespoon ruby port or sweet or dry sherry (optional)

1 Put the water and sugar into a pan and heat until the sugar dissolves.

2 Add the cranberries and bring to the boil. Reduce the heat, cover the pan and simmer for about 15 minutes until the cranberries have burst and are tender.

3 Add the port and sherry, if using, and stir in.

4 Transfer the boiling sauce to hot dry jars leaving a headspace of 2.5 cm (1 inch). Cover the surface of each with a disc of waxed paper, waxed side down, then cover with a screw-topped lid or clips. If using screw bands give a half turn back to allow for the expansion of the tops of the jars. Stand a small wire rack in the bottom of a deep pan and fill the pan with boiling water. Put the jars on the rack and boil for 5–8 minutes.

5 Ladle some of the water out of the pan, then, using oven gloves, carefully lift the jars out on to a wooden board and leave to cool. When cold, check the jar seals (see page 13). Label and store, unopened, for up to 6 months.

Spiced plum sauce
An oriental-inspired sweet and sour sauce made with a vinegar base and flavoured with star anise, five-spice powder and chilli. Serve with roast duck, grilled pork chops or add to vegetable stir-fries.

MAKES: 1 litre (1¾ pints)

PREPARATION TIME: 15 minutes

COOKING TIME: 30 minutes

- **1 kg (2 lb) red plums, halved, pitted and roughly chopped**
- **300 g (10 oz) caster sugar**
- **500 ml (17 fl oz) red wine vinegar**
- **3 star anise**
- **½ teaspoon five-spice powder**
- **1 dried red chilli, halved**
- **1 teaspoon salt**
- **½ teaspoon coarsely crushed black peppercorns**

1 Put all the ingredients into a large pan and stir to combine. Slowly bring to the boil, stirring occasionally, until the sugar has dissolved. Reduce the heat, cover the pan and simmer for 30 minutes until the plums are soft.

2 Press the mixture through a sieve into a large jug and discard the spices and fruit skins. Transfer the hot sauce to dry bottles, leaving a headspace of 2.5 cm (1 inch). Add lids and seal loosely. Stand a small wire rack in the bottom of a deep pan and put the bottles, spaced slightly apart, on the rack. Pour warm water into the pan to come up to the neck of the bottles.

3 Slowly bring the water to a temperature of 88°C (190°F) on a sugar thermometer over 1 hour, or until the sauce is just simmering, but not boiling. Maintain the temperature for 30 minutes.

4 Ladle some of the water out of the pan, then, using tongs, carefully lift the bottles out on to a wooden board. Using a cloth, tighten the seal on the lids and leave to cool. Label and store in a cool, dark place. It will keep for 3–6 months. Serve the sauce warm or cold. Once opened, store in the refrigerator for up to 2 weeks.

Fruit, flowers, nuts and vegetables

Syrups, oils and vinegars can also be used to great effect to capture nature's bounty. Here we show how to crystallize flowers and make marrons glacés, glacé fruits and crystallized ginger by soaking them in a rich sugar syrup, and how to use flavoured sugar syrup to bottle fruits, for the perfect winter delicacy or Christmas gift. They are not difficult to make, but do take a little time to pack into the jars and a watchful eye while cooking. Or for something speedier, alcohol-steeped fruits make a wonderful accompaniment to vanilla ice cream.

Vinegar may be used to preserve diverse ingredients from chillies to walnuts, ginger and gherkins to garlic, while oil can be used to marinate and preserve cheeses, artichokes and olives, layered with herbs, peppercorns and pared fruit rinds.

Glacé fruits

Glacé fruits are expensive to buy, but they aren't difficult to prepare yourself. Although the process is lengthy, it is worth the effort as they can be really delicious – use them in cakes, breads and sweets or to decorate desserts.

PREPARATION TIME: 15 minutes

COOKING TIME: over a period of 8 days

pineapple, sliced and then quartered

cherries, pitted but kept whole

firm pears, peeled, cored and halved

plums, stoned and halved

apricots, stoned and halved

granulated sugar

1 Cook all the fruit gently in water to cover until just tender.

2 For each 500 g (1 lb) of fruit allow 300 ml (½ pint) of syrup. Make this by combining 300 ml (½ pint) of the water in which the fruits were cooked with 175 g (6 oz) sugar. Stir over a low heat until the sugar has dissolved.

3 Put the cooked fruit in a single layer in a shallow dish and pour over the warm syrup. Cover the dish and leave for 24 hours.

4 On day 2, drain the syrup from the fruit and measure into a pan. Add 50 g (2 oz) sugar for each 300 ml (½ pint) of syrup and bring to the boil. Pour over the fruit, cover and leave for 24 hours.

5 Repeat this 3 times – each time adding an additional 50 g (2 oz) sugar to the syrup.

6 On day 6, drain the fruit, return the syrup to the pan and add 75 g (3 oz) sugar for each 300 ml (½ pint) of syrup. Bring to the boil, add the fruit and boil for 3 minutes. Return to the dish and leave for 24 hours.

7 Repeat step 6. The syrup should be like thick honey. If it is thin, repeat once again.

8 Drain the syrup and arrange the fruit in a single layer on a wire rack set over a baking sheet. Leave to dry. Store in an airtight box between layers of waxed paper.

Crystallized ginger *An ideal gift for a real foodie.*

*For an impressive petit four, dip crystallized ginger into chocolate
or slice and use to decorate gingerbreads.*

MAKES: 250 g (8 oz)

PREPARATION TIME: 1 hour

COOKING TIME: over a period of 11–12 days

500 g (1 lb) fresh root ginger, trimmed
300 ml (½ pint) water
625 g (1¼ lb) granulated sugar
25 g (1 oz) caster sugar

1 Cut the ginger into large manageable chunks and peel. Cut into 1 cm (½ inch) thick slices and cut any very wide slices in half again. Put into a pan with the water, bring to the boil, then reduce the heat, cover and simmer for 25–30 minutes until just tender.

2 Drain the ginger and water into a sieve set over a measuring jug. Top up the water to the original amount if necessary. Return the water to the pan and add 250 g (8 oz) of the granulated sugar. Cook over a low heat, stirring continuously, until the sugar has completely dissolved, then boil for 2 minutes.

3 Put the ginger into a small bowl and pour the syrup over to cover completely. Cover and leave in a warm place overnight.

4 On day 2, strain the syrup back into the pan and add 50 g (2 oz) more of the sugar. Heat gently until dissolved, then boil for 1 minute. Pour back over the ginger, cover and leave overnight.

5 Repeat on days 3, 4, 5, 6 and 7 until all the granulated sugar has been added to the syrup. Leave the ginger to soak for 48 hours.

6 On day 9, boil the ginger and syrup for 3–5 minutes until the syrup is very thick, then lift the ginger out of the syrup and arrange in a single layer on a wire rack set over a baking sheet. Leave in a warm place for 2–3 days to dry out, turning once so that the ginger dries evenly.

7 On day 11/12, fill a small bowl with boiling water and put the caster sugar on a plate. Using a fork, dip each piece of ginger into the boiling water, shake off excess water, then roll in the caster sugar. Leave to dry for 12 hours, then pack into a greaseproof-lined airtight tin. Label and store in a cool, dark place. It will keep for up to 3 months.

Tips

• There are two ways of making crystallized or glacé fruits – one is to add extra sugar each day, the other is to boil the syrup each day so that it reduces. Either way the idea is that the sugar syrup gets more concentrated until the fruits become saturated with the syrup.

• Don't try to hurry the process; although it seems spread out over a number of days, it really only takes 5 minutes each day with just a few extra minutes on days 9 and 12.

Crystallized flowers
Use only edible flowers and blossoms. Non-edible flowers are those that come from bulbs – in many cases these are poisonous.

PREPARATION TIME: 15 minutes, plus picking and standing

25 g (1 oz) gum arabic

triple strength rosewater

edible flowers: roses, violets, primroses, shaken out to clean

blossoms: plum, cherry, apple, pear, heather, shaken out to clean

caster sugar

1 Cover the gum arabic with the rosewater and leave for 24 hours to dissolve completely.

2 Using a fine paint brush, paint each petal of the flowers or blossoms all over on both sides with the gum arabic water. Then, holding each flower or blossom by the stem, sprinkle all over with caster sugar.

3 Leave the flowers or blossoms to dry on sheets of greaseproof paper, then store in an airtight tin.

Marrons glacés

A French favourite, made by slowly soaking cooked fresh chestnuts in vanilla syrup until almost translucent, these are wonderful served with after-dinner coffee or used to decorate chocolate desserts.

MAKES: 60 pieces

PREPARATION TIME: 40 minutes

COOKING TIME: over a period of 9–10 days

500 g (1 lb) sweet chestnuts
250 g (8 oz) granulated sugar
250 g (8 oz) liquid glucose
300 ml (½ pint) water
½ teaspoon vanilla extract

For the glacé finish:
125 g (4 oz) granulated sugar
3 tablespoons water

1 Cut a small cross in the top of each chestnut. Place in a pan of boiling water and cook for 2 minutes. Take off the heat and, using a slotted spoon, scoop out 8–10 chestnuts at a time into a teacloth. Using a small knife, peel away the hard outer skin and thinner inner skin of each. Return any stubborn chestnuts to the water, bring back to the boil, then try again. Discard any damaged or blackened nuts.

2 Put the chestnuts back into the drained and dried pan and add cold water to cover them well. Bring to the boil, then reduce the heat and simmer gently, uncovered, for 20 minutes until just tender but still firm. Do not overcook them or the chestnuts will break up. Drain and transfer to a shallow dish.

3 Put the sugar, liquid glucose and water into a pan. Heat gently until the sugar has completely dissolved, then boil for 1 minute. Pour over the chestnuts, cover and leave in a warm place overnight.

4 On day 2, drain the syrup back into the pan and boil for 4 minutes. Pour over the chestnuts, cover and leave overnight as before.

5 On day 3, repeat as day 2, adding the vanilla essence after boiling.

6 On day 4, repeat the sugar boiling process. Add the chestnuts and leave to soak for 3 days.

7 On day 7, lift the chestnuts out of the pan and arrange in a single layer on a wire rack set over a baking sheet. Leave in a warm place for 2–3 days to dry them, turning once or twice until the coating is hard.

8 On day 9–10, make the glacé finish. Heat the water and sugar gently until the sugar has completely dissolved, then boil for 1 minute to make a syrup. Using tongs, dip each chestnut into boiling water, then shake off excess water and dip into the sugar syrup. For best results pour a little of the sugar syrup into a bowl and use this for dipping, topping it up as needed so that the syrup doesn't get cloudy with any pieces of chestnut.

9 Arrange the chestnuts in a single layer on a wire rack set over a baking sheet and leave to dry in a cool place overnight. Wrap in foil or arrange in foil petits fours cases and store in an airtight tin. Keep in a cool, dry place for up to 3 months.

Tip

• It is crucial that the marrons glacés are kept well away from any moisture or they will quickly spoil.

Peaches in marsala wine
Serve these peaches, either cold or gently warmed, spooned into bowls and topped with good-quality vanilla ice cream, or spoonfuls of crème fraîche mixed with crumbled ratafia biscuits.

MAKES: 1 kg (2 lb)

PREPARATION TIME: 5 minutes, plus cooling

COOKING TIME: 2 hours

125 g (4 oz) caster sugar

300 ml (½ pint) water

7–8 small firm peaches

150 ml (¼ pint) marsala wine

½ teaspoon citric acid

1 Put the sugar and water into a pan and cook over a low heat, stirring continuously, until the sugar has completely dissolved. Increase the heat and bring to the boil, then cook for 1 minute. Take off the heat and leave the syrup to cool.

2 Peel, halve and stone the peaches, adding to acidulated water as you work (see page 12), so that the peaches don't discolour.

3 Using a slotted spoon, carefully lift the peaches out of the water and pack tightly into jars, so that they tuck one inside the other and stand up in single layer.

4 Stir the wine and citric acid into the cold sugar syrup, then pour over the fruit to cover completely and to come almost to the brim of the jars. Top up with cold previously boiled water from the kettle if needed and seal with airtight tops.

5 Stand a small wire rack in the bottom of a large deep pan and put the jars on top, then pour cold water into the pan to submerge the jars. Slowly bring the water to 55°C (130°F) on a sugar thermometer over the course of 1 hour. Over the next 30 minutes gradually increase the temperature to 82°C (180°F), then maintain this temperature for a further 15 minutes.

6 Ladle some of the water out of the pan, then, using oven gloves, carefully lift the jars out on to a wooden board and leave to cool. When cold, check the jar seals (see page 12). Label and leave to mature in a cool, dark place for 3–4 weeks before using, or store, unopened, for 6–12 months.

Variation
The same method can be used for apricots in Amaretto liqueur, and plums or peaches in brandy.

Tips
• Even when they are tightly shut, some air can escape from Le Parfait jars during heating, this is vital or the jars may explode. If using kilner jars, tighten the metal ring, then release slightly.

• Keep an eye on the temperature and try to adjust the heat so that the temperature rises slowly. If you overheat the water at the beginning, don't be tempted to cut down on the cooking time. If the heat is too rapid then the fruit will be overcooked and will lose colour.

Blueberries in kirsch
Quick and simple to prepare yet deliciously indulgent to eat spooned over vanilla ice cream or pancakes and crème fraîche; or fold into whipped cream for a special cake filling.

MAKES: 400 g (13 oz)
PREPARATION TIME: 10 minutes, plus standing

175 g (6 oz) blueberries, destalked
50 g (2 oz) caster sugar
100 ml (3½ fl oz) kirsch

1 Pick over the blueberries, discarding any very soft ones. Prick each berry with a fork, then layer in a clean dry jar, sprinkling each layer with some sugar.

2 Pour over the kirsch. Seal tightly and shake once or twice.

3 Leave in a cool place and turn the jar upside down every day for 4 days until the sugar has completely dissolved. Label and leave to mature in a cool, dark place for 3–4 weeks before using, or store, unopened, for 6–12 months.

Variation
You can also make this with fresh red or black pitted cherries.

Figs in vanilla syrup

Fresh figs are in season for only a short time and, unlike many summer fruits, do not freeze well when baked in tarts or pies. Capture their full flavour by bottling in a rich vanilla syrup.

MAKES: 500 g (1 lb)
PREPARATION TIME: 20 minutes
COOKING TIME: 35–40 minutes

8–9 firm fresh figs, halved
100 g (4 oz) caster sugar
400 ml (7 fl oz) water
½ vanilla pod, slit lengthways
½ teaspoon citric acid

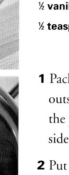

1 Pack the figs with the cut sides facing the outside of a warm jar. Pack the centre of the jar tightly and put two halves, cut side uppermost, in the top of the jar.

2 Put the sugar, water and vanilla pod into a pan. Slowly bring to the boil and heat, stirring continuously, until the sugar has completely dissolved. Boil for 1 minute, then remove from the heat.

3 Lift the vanilla pod out of the syrup and, using a small knife, scrape out the black seeds into the syrup and stir in the citric acid. Tuck the vanilla pod down the side of the jar.

4 Pour the syrup over the figs to cover completely and come almost to the brim of the jar. Top up with boiling water if needed and seal the jar. Stand the jar on a baking sheet lined with several sheets of folded newspaper and bake in a preheated oven, 150°C (300°F), Gas 2, for 40 minutes until the syrup has turned a delicate pink and the figs are just beginning to rise in the jar.

5 Using oven gloves, transfer the jar to a wooden board, close the clasp fully and leave to cool completely. When cold, check the jar seals (see page 12). Label and store in a cool, dark place. The figs will keep for 6–12 months.

Dill pickles
This pickle is best made in midsummer, when gherkins are plentiful. This recipe really needs thick stalks and flower heads as well as leaves, so home-grown dill is infinitely better than that sold in the shops.

MAKES: 1 kg (2 lb)

PREPARATION TIME: 5 minutes

COOKING TIME: 5 minutes

1 kg (2 lb) gherkins or small cucumbers (or halved cucumbers cut into wedges), washed and dried

2 garlic cloves, thinly sliced

12 large sprigs of dill, including flowers if possible

3 bay leaves

For the pickle:

750 ml (1¼ pints) water

250 ml (8 fl oz) vinegar

25 g (1 oz) sea salt

12 black peppercorns

12 allspice berries

1 Layer the gherkins (or cucumbers or wedges) into a 1 kg (2 lb) glass preserving jar, sprinkling each layer with the garlic, dill and bay leaves.

2 Put all the ingredients for the pickle into a pan, bring to the boil and boil for 3 minutes, then leave to cool and pour over the gherkins.

3 Top the pickle with an airtight lid. Label and leave to mature in a cool, dark place for 2 weeks before using, or store, unopened, for up to 3 months.

Fennel and chilli-marinated olives

If you don't have a good delicatessen near you selling tasty olives, then buy loose olives in brine from the supermarket and jazz them up with this tasty marinade.

MAKES: 500 g (1 lb)

PREPARATION TIME: 15 minutes

COOKING TIME: 2 minutes

200 ml (7fl oz) virgin olive oil

4 garlic cloves, thinly sliced

1 tablespoon fennel seeds, roughly crushed

2 dried red chillies, deseeded, if preferred, and roughly crushed

300 g (10 oz) Kalamata olives in brine

½ red onion, finely chopped

1 teaspoon multi-coloured peppercorns

a little salt

1 Heat 2 tablespoons of the oil in a nonstick frying pan and add the garlic, fennel seeds and chillies and cook for 1 minute.

2 Drain the olives, prick each one with a skewer or fork and put into a bowl.

3 Add the onion to the olives with the fried seeds, chillies, garlic, peppercorns and salt. Mix together well.

4 Spoon the olive mixture into clean dry jars and top up with the remaining oil so that the olives are completely covered. Top with airtight lids, then label and store in a cool, dark place. They will keep for up to 3 months.

Tip

• Use any remaining flavoured oil in salad dressings or pasta dishes, or brush over barbecue meats or when frying meat or fish.

Marinated goats' cheese with chilli pepper and basil

These jars of attractively layered slices of goats' cheese dipped in crushed chillies, peppercorns and coarse sea salt make great gourmet gifts.

MAKES: 450 g (14½ oz)

PREPARATION TIME: 20 minutes

2 goats' cheeses, each 100 g (3½ oz)

2 teaspoons multi-coloured peppercorns, roughly crushed

1 teaspoon coarse sea salt, roughly crushed

1 teaspoon dried chilli seeds

50 g (2 oz) black olives

small bunch of basil leaves

250 ml (8 fl oz) virgin olive oil

1 Cut off and discard the rind from the top and bottom of each cheese, then cut the cheese into thin slices and cut each slice in half again.

2 Mix together the peppercorns, salt and chilli seeds together and tip on to a plate. Dip the cut sides of the cheese into the chilli mixture until lightly coated.

3 Layer the cheese, olives and whole basil leaves into clean dry jars. Top up with the olive oil and, using the back of a teaspoon, press the cheese gently under the surface of the oil, if necessary. Top with airtight lids, then label and store in the refrigerator for up to 1 month.

Marinated goats' cheese with chilli pepper and basil

Marinated feta cheese
Bring back memories of hot balmy Mediterranean days with these tasty cubes of lemony marinated feta cheese. Serve with warm crusty bread, or spoon over crisp salad leaves for lunch.

MAKES: 800 g (1 lb 10 oz)

PREPARATION TIME: 20 minutes

250 g (8 oz) feta cheese, drained and cut into cubes

1 small bunch of lemon thyme, leaves stripped from stems

grated rind of 1 lemon

4 teaspoons drained capers

1 teaspoon multi-coloured peppercorns, roughly crushed

½ red onion, thinly sliced

400 ml (14 fl oz) virgin olive oil

1 Put the feta, 4 tablespoons of the thyme leaves, the lemon rind, capers and peppercorns into a bowl and mix together gently with a large spoon.

2 Spoon the cheese mixture and sliced onion into two clean dry jars. Top up with the olive oil and, using the back of a teaspoon, press the cheese beneath the surface of the oil, if necessary. Top with airtight lids. Label and leave to mature in a cool, dark place for 2 weeks before using, or store, unopened, for about 6 months.

3 To serve, spoon the feta into a bowl and leave at room temperature for about 1 hour to enable the flavours to fully develop.

Variation
Try with sun-dried tomatoes, rosemary and garlic or chilli, basil and fennel seeds or experiment and make up your own variation.

Pickled red peppers
These vegetables are useful ingredients in salads, pizzas and sauces. You can also add them to well-flavoured casseroles, but be careful not to make the result vinegary.

MAKES: 4

PREPARATION TIME: 10 minutes

COOKING TIME: 15 hours

4 red peppers

600 ml (1 pint) white vinegar

225 g (8 oz) sugar

1 tablespoon salt

1 Cut the tops off the peppers and scoop out all the pith and seeds. Blanch them in boiling water for about 3 minutes or until just soft. Dry them well on absorbent kitchen paper.

2 Pour the vinegar into a saucepan, add the sugar and salt and bring the mixture to the boil. Cover the pan and simmer for 10 minutes.

3 Pack the peppers into dry jars and strain in the hot vinegar, making sure that the peppers are completely covered, then top with airtight lids. Label and leave to mature for 1 week. The peppers can be stored for up to 6 months.

Preserved lemons
Preserved lemons are a vital ingredient in many Moroccan stews. They are indispensable for the sharp flavour and soft texture they impart, which is impossible to replicate.

MAKES: 4

PREPARATION TIME: 10 minutes

4 unwaxed lemons

50 g (2 oz) sea salt

1 teaspoon coriander seeds

1 small cinnamon stick, bruised

2 bay leaves

juice of 1 lemon

1 Cut the lemons into 6 wedges, but leave attached at one end. Sprinkle some of the salt into the incisions.

2 Sprinkle a little of the remaining salt into the bottom of a large, wide-necked jar, then layer the lemons, spices, bay leaves and salt in the jar.

3 Add any remaining salt, the lemon juice and enough boiling water to cover the lemons. Top with an airtight lid and leave in a warm place for at least 2 weeks before using, for the lemon skins to soften. Once opened, the lemons can be stored for up to 12 months. A white lacy film may appear on the jar or on the lemons – this is harmless and can be rinsed off.

Herby pickled plums

Pickled plums are delicious served with cold meats, salad and a jacket potato. They also make an ideal present if a few extra herbs are tied decoratively on the clip of the jar with ribbon or raffia.

MAKES: 2 kg (4 lb)

PREPARATION TIME: 20 minutes

COOKING TIME: 2–2½ hours

750 ml (1¼ pints) white wine vinegar

500 g (1 lb) caster sugar

7 rosemary sprigs

7 thyme sprigs

7 small bay leaves

4 lavender sprigs (optional)

4 garlic cloves, unpeeled

1 teaspoon salt

½ teaspoon multi-coloured peppercorns

1.5 kg (3 lb) firm red plums, washed and pricked

1 Use a standard slow cooker and preheat if necessary. Pour the vinegar and sugar into the cooker pot and add 4 each of the rosemary and thyme sprigs and bay leaves, all the lavender, if using, the garlic, salt and peppercorns. Cook on 'High' for 2–2½ hours, stirring once or twice.

2 Warm the clean jars in the bottom of a low oven. Pack the plums tightly into the warm dry jars and tuck the remaining fresh herbs into them. Strain in the hot vinegar, making sure that the plums are completely covered, then top with airtight lids.

3 Label and leave to mature in a cool, dark place for 3–4 weeks before using, or store, unopened, for 6–12 months. The plums will lose colour slightly.

Variation

Add a tiny dried chilli to each jar of plums or use some broken cinnamon sticks, juniper berries and pared orange rind in place of the fresh herbs.

Pickled garlic
Many people assume that garlic always has a very strong, intense flavour, but this mellows over time. Pickled garlic can be added to meat and vegetable dishes or stocks, or try them by themselves.

MAKES: 6 garlic heads
PREPARATION TIME: 30 minutes
COOKING TIME: 10 minutes, plus cooling

1.2 litres (2 pints) water
300 ml (½ pint) distilled white wine vinegar
50 g (2 oz) granulated sugar
1 tablespoon salt
6 heads of garlic, separated into cloves and peeled

1 Bring the water, vinegar, sugar and salt to the boil in a pan, then reduce the heat and simmer for 5 minutes.

2 Add the garlic to the pan, return to the boil and boil hard for 1 minute.

3 Remove the pan from the heat, allow the garlic mixture to cool, then transfer to containers and top with airtight lids. Label and leave to mature in the refrigerator for 10 days before using, or store, unopened, for 6 months.

Sweet pickled ginger
Although root ginger stores well unpeeled, pickling removes fiddly preparation. Use in any Thai or Chinese-style stir fry or Japanese nori-wrapped sushi.

MAKES: 500 g (1 Ib) or 2 small jars
PREPARATION TIME: 20 minutes, plus standing
COOKING TIME: 10 minutes

275 g (9 oz) fresh root ginger, peeled and cut into wafer-thin slices
50 g (2 oz) coarse sea salt
250 ml (9 fl oz) rice vinegar
100 g (3½ oz) caster sugar
2 Thai red chillies, thinly sliced
a few white peppercorns

1 Layer the ginger in a dish with the salt, cover with a plate and leave to stand for 24 hours.

2 Pour the vinegar into a saucepan, add the sugar and heat gently until dissolved. Add the sliced chilli and peppercorns and simmer for 5 minutes.

3 Meanwhile, put the ginger into a sieve and rinse with cold water to remove the salt then drain and pat dry with kitchen paper.

4 Pack the slices of ginger into two dry jars and pour over the hot vinegar and flavourings, making sure that the ginger is completely covered. Top with airtight lids, label and leave to cool. The ginger can be stored in a cool dark place for up to 6 months.

Tip
• If you don't have any fresh chillies, use 1 large dried red chilli.

Pickled walnuts

Use only young walnuts for this recipe; if they are over-ripe they will not pickle. Serve with both cold meats and most varieties of cheese – the textures of ripe Brie or Camembert are very complementary.

MAKES: about 2 litres (3 pints)
PREPARATION TIME: 10 minutes, plus soaking and standing
COOKING TIME: 15 minutes

500 g (1 lb) young fresh walnuts
50 g (2 oz) salt
600 ml (1 pint) water
3 level teaspoons mixed pickling spice
1.7 litres (3 pints) white wine vinegar

1 Using a silver fork, prick each walnut deeply in 2 or 3 places.

2 To make the brine, add the salt to the water and stir to mix. Add the walnuts, ensuring they are covered in the brine, place a plate on top to keep them submerged and soak them for 14 days.

3 Remove the walnuts from the brine and place on a tray or cloth in the sun, shaking them occasionally. They will turn black after 2 or 3 days, or in 24 hours if it is very hot.

4 Meanwhile, make the spiced vinegar. Put the mixed pickling spice and vinegar into a pan and boil for 15 minutes. Strain and leave until cold.

5 When the walnuts are quite black, pack into jars and cover with the spiced vinegar. Top with airtight lids. Label and leave to mature in a cool, dark place for at least 1 month before using, or store, unopened, for 3–4 months.

Oils, butters and vinegars *Transform plain oils and vinegars into gourmet ingredients by steeping with herbs, spices, fruits or aromatics. Since no cooking or heat processing is required they are quick to prepare — the secret is in the time that you leave the flavours to develop. Nuts and flowers require just a few days, while herbs, garlic, chillies and other flavourings can be left for two weeks. Strain into pretty bottles and add one or two ingredients to illustrate the flavouring.*

If you are packing oils and vinegars as a gift, conceal ordinary gold- or silver-coloured screw-topped lids with muslin squares or waxed paper and tie in place with string or raffia, or cover the lid by binding it with string and seal the ends with candle wax or coloured sealing wax. Give suggestions for using the oil or vinegar on labels.

Strawberry and pink peppercorn vinegar

Capture the very essence of summer with this light, delicately flavoured vinegar. Add to salad dressings or use when frying calves' liver.

MAKES: 2 x 500 ml (17 fl oz) bottles

PREPARATION TIME: 15 minutes, plus standing

300 g (10 oz) strawberries, hulled and cut into quarters

1 tablespoon pink peppercorns in brine, drained and roughly crushed

1 litre (1¾ pints) white wine vinegar

a few extra strawberries and pink peppercorns, to finish

1 Put the strawberries into a clean dry wide-necked bottle or glass storage jar. Add the peppercorns and top up with the vinegar. Seal with an airtight top and turn the bottle upside down several times to bruise the strawberries slightly and to release their flavour.

2 Leave in a warm place for 2 weeks, turning the bottle once a day.

3 Transfer the vinegar to dry bottles and tuck a few extra whole strawberries and peppercorns into the bottles to decorate. Seal with airtight tops, then label and store in a cool, dark place. The vinegar will keep for up to 6 months.

Variation

A small handful of edible flowers can also be used to flavour vinegars and oils, or use a combination of flowers and herbs. Pansies or nasturtium flowers could also be added, but reduce the storage time to 3 months.

Walnut vinegar

A real gourmet treat that can be made for a fraction of the cost of its shop-bought equivalent. Add to salad dressings, beef casseroles and game dishes.

MAKES: 2 x 250 ml (8 fl oz) bottles

PREPARATION TIME: 15 minutes, plus standing

200 g (7 oz) walnut pieces
600 ml (1 pint) red wine vinegar
1 tablespoon clear honey

1 Put the walnuts into a large clean dry storage jar and top up with the vinegar.

2 Seal tightly and leave at room temperature for 4 days, turning the jar upside down each day.

3 Strain the vinegar through a fine sieve to remove all sediment. Stir in the honey, then transfer to dry bottles. (As walnuts are high in oil they reduce the storage life of the flavoured vinegar, so don't add extra nuts to the finished vinegar.)

4 Seal with airtight tops, then label and store in a cool, dark place. The vinegar will keep for up to 3 months.

Raspberry vinegar
This is a good way to use up any fruit that might be squashed at the bottom of the basket. Use as the basis of dressings with salads, or mix a little with sugar and hot water for a winter drink.

PREPARATION TIME: 5 minutes, plus standing

COOKING TIME: 10 minutes

ripe raspberries
white malt vinegar
sugar

1 Put the raspberries into a glass bowl. For each 500 g (1 lb) of fruit add 600 ml (1 pint) of vinegar.

2 Leave for 3–5 days, stirring occasionally.

3 Strain the liquid and measure it into a pan. Add 250 g–500 g (8 oz–1 lb) sugar for each 600 ml (1 pint) of liquid, depending on how sweet you like it.

4 Boil for 10 minutes, then transfer to hot dry bottles. Seal with airtight tops, then label and leave to cool. Store in a cool, dark place. The vinegar will keep for up to 12 months.

Tarragon vinegar
The delicate flavour of tarragon makes one of the best of all the flavoured vinegars. Try it as a dressing for fish salads or use it in béarnaise and hollandaise sauces.

PREPARATION TIME: 15 minutes, plus standing

tarragon leaves
malt or white vinegar

1 Bruise the tarragon leaves by crushing them with a rolling pin, to extract their flavour, then pack them into jars, half filling each jar.

2 Pour the vinegar over the tarragon and seal the jars with airtight tops.

3 Leave in a cool place for 6 weeks, shaking the bottles once a day.

4 Strain the vinegar through a fine sieve to remove all sediment, then transfer to dry bottles. Seal with airtight tops, then label and store in a cool, dark place. It will keep for up to 3 months.

Hot chilli and garlic oil

A fiery oil that packs a punch when used in stir-fries and salad dressings, or to marinate beef or fish. The oil is also great served in small bowls with warmed bread to dunk into it.

MAKES: 2 x 500 ml (17 fl oz) bottles

PREPARATION TIME: 15 minutes, plus standing

1 litre (1¾ pints) virgin olive oil

10 large dried red chillies, halved, deseeded, if preferred, and cut into 4 pieces

10 garlic cloves, roughly chopped

2 teaspoons black peppercorns, roughly crushed

a few extra chillies, to decorate

1 Heat a little of the oil in a nonstick frying pan, add the chillies and garlic and cook for 1 minute to release their flavour.

2 Pour the remaining oil into a large, clean, dry wide-necked storage jar, then add the chillies, garlic and the frying oil and the peppercorns. Seal tightly and leave in a warm place for 2 weeks.

3 Strain the oil through a fine sieve to remove all sediment, then transfer to dry bottles. Halve a few extra chillies (deseed, if preferred) and tuck into the bottles to decorate. Seal with airtight tops, then label and store in a cool, dark place. It will keep for up to 6 months.

Lemon grass and kaffir lime oil *Infused with Thai flavourings and spices, this light fresh-tasting oil is delicious added to rice noodle or prawn salads, or as a speedy flavour-enhancer to any stir-fry.*

MAKES: 2 x 500 ml (17 fl oz) bottles

PREPARATION TIME: 15 minutes, plus standing

COOKING TIME: 2 minutes

1 litre (1¾ pints) sunflower oil

5 cm (2 inch) piece of fresh root ginger, peeled and chopped

6 garlic cloves, roughly chopped

2 stems lemon grass, quartered

10 dried kaffir lime leaves

10 small fresh Thai red chillies, halved and deseeded

rind of 2 limes

extra lemon grass, red chillies, deseeded if preferred, lime leaves and lime rind, to finish

1 Heat 2 tablespoons of the oil in a nonstick frying pan, add the ginger and garlic and cook for 1 minute. Bruise the lemon grass with a pestle, then add to the pan with the lime leaves and chillies. Cook for 1 minute.

2 Put the lime rind into a clean, dry wide-necked storage jar. Pour the remaining oil over it, then spoon in the hot spices and stir well.

3 Seal the jar tightly and leave in a warm place for 2 weeks, turning the jar upside down each day.

4 Strain the oil through a fine sieve to remove all sediment, then transfer the oil to dry bottles and tuck a few extra flavourings into the bottles to decorate. Seal with airtight tops, then label and store in a cool, dark place. It will keep for up to 6 months.

Tip

• Always be careful when preparing chillies as they can make your eyes smart and stream with water if you touch them without realising it. Wash your hands as soon as you have finished preparing them or wear rubber gloves.

Mediterranean herb oil
This flavoursome oil is a great way to use herbs from your garden. Pick fresh herbs after the dew has dried and before the heat of the day. If the herbs are damp, it may cause the oil to go mouldy.

MAKES: 2 x 500 ml (17 fl oz) bottles

PREPARATION TIME: 15 minutes, plus standing

1 large handful of mixed herbs to include rosemary, thyme and marjoram, or a single variety such as rosemary, tarragon or thyme

1 litre (1¾ pints) virgin olive oil

extra fresh herbs, to finish

1 Put the herbs into a large, clean, dry wide-necked storage jar and top up with the oil.

2 Seal tightly and turn the jar upside down several times to bruise the leaves slightly and to release their flavouring oils.

3 Leave the jar in a warm place for 2 weeks, turning it once a day.

4 Strain the oil through a fine sieve to remove all sediment, then transfer the oil to dry bottles and tuck a few herb sprigs into the bottles to decorate. Seal with airtight tops, then label and store in a cool, dark place. It will keep for up to 6 months.

Provençal butters

Although one associates the south of France with olive oil, butter is used in many dishes and is often flavoured with locally grown herbs and aromatics.

PREPARATION TIME: 5 minutes, for each butter

For each butter:

100 g (4 oz) unsalted butter, at room temperature

2–4 teaspoons olive oil

Saffron flavouring:

1 teaspoon saffron threads

large pinch of sea salt

Basil and garlic flavouring:

30 g (1 oz) basil leaves

2 garlic cloves, crushed

a squeeze of lemon juice

salt and freshly ground black pepper

Anchoïade flavouring:

50 g (2 oz) pitted black olives, chopped

4 salted anchovy fillets, drained and chopped

freshly ground black pepper

To serve:

young radishes

sliced French sticks

sea salt and freshly ground black pepper

1 To make the saffron butter, grind the saffron threads with the sea salt to a powder using a mortar and pestle. Then purée with the butter and olive oil.

2 To make the basil and garlic butter and anchoïade butter, combine the ingredients for each in a food processor and process until smooth.

3 Roll each butter into a log, then wrap in clingfilm or greaseproof paper. Chill until required, then serve with the radishes, bread and salt and pepper.

Cordials, syrups and liqueurs

Generally, cordials and syrups are the same thing and are made by poaching fruits in a little water, then straining and sweetening to taste. To lengthen storage times, the bottles of concentrate must be heat-treated in a similar way to bottled fruits. If you use produce from your garden or allotment they are economical to make. Always dilute them before use with chilled water, fizzy lemonade or tonic water, or chilled dry or sparkling white wine.

Home-made liqueurs are simple to make. As alcohol has such good preservative qualities, the fruits and flavourings do not require any cooking or heat processing. Simply place fruit in clean dry wide-necked bottles, sweeten to taste and cover with a complementary spirit, such as gin with sloes, brandy with apricots or vodka with strawberries. Then leave the flavours to mature without being tempted to sample the goodies!

Lavender and redcurrant syrup

For a refreshing summer party drink, mix one part syrup to four parts well-chilled dry sparkling wine or sparkling mineral water.

MAKES: 3 x 250 ml (8 fl oz) bottles
PREPARATION TIME: 25 minutes, plus standing and straining
COOKING TIME: 2–2¼ hours

1.5 kg (3 lb) redcurrants, destemmed
300 ml (½ pint) water
12 large fresh or dried lavender heads
about 375 g (12 oz) granulated sugar

1 Put the redcurrants into a pan with the water and crush with a potato masher. Cover and cook over a low heat for 30 minutes. Take the pan off the heat and crush the fruits again. Add the lavender heads and press them down beneath the liquid. Leave to infuse for 1 hour, then strain the mixture overnight through a jelly bag suspended over a large bowl.

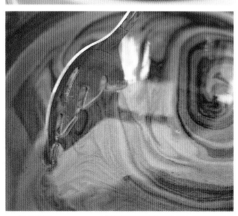

2 The next day, measure the juice into a large pan and add 375 g (12 oz) sugar for each 600 ml (1 pint) of juice. Cook over a low heat, stirring continuously, for about 10 minutes until the sugar has dissolved.

3 Skim off any scum. Transfer the syrup to dry bottles, leaving a headspace of 2.5 cm (1 inch). Add tops and seal loosely. Stand the bottles on a wire rack in a deep pan with newspaper wedged between them to hold them in place. Then fill the pan with cold water up to the necks of the bottles.

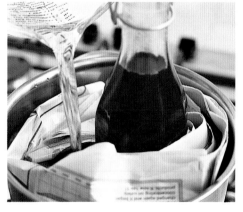

4 Put a sugar thermometer into the pan and slowly heat the water over 1 hour to 77°C (170°F), then maintain the temperature for 20–30 minutes depending on the size of the bottles.

5 Using tongs, carefully lift the jars out on to a wooden board. Seal the tops and leave to cool. Label and store in a cool, dark place for up to 3–6 months.

Lavender and redcurrant syrup

Elderflower and lemon cordial

This cordial is wonderfully refreshing, tangy and aromatic and is very cheap to make. Pick elderflowers from field hedgerows just as they come into blossom.

MAKES: 3 x 500 ml (17 fl oz) and 1 x 250 ml (8 fl oz) bottles

PREPARATION TIME: 20 minutes, plus standing and straining

COOKING TIME: 10 minutes

12 elderflower heads, shaken and picked over

grated rind of 2 lemons

grated rind of 1 orange

1.5 litres (2½ pints) freshly boiled water

875 g (1¾ lb) granulated sugar

juice of 5 lemons or 200 ml (7 fl oz) lemon juice

25 g (1 oz) tartaric acid

1 Rinse a large bowl with boiling water, then add the elderflowers and lemon and orange rinds. Cover with the freshly boiled water and press the flowerheads beneath the water, keeping them down if needs be with crumpled, wetted greaseproof paper. Cover the bowl and leave to stand overnight.

2 The next day, pour the water, flowers and fruit rinds through a fine sieve or jelly bag suspended over a large bowl. Leave to drip for 30 minutes.

3 Pour the liquid into a large pan and add the sugar and lemon juice. Cook over a low heat, stirring continuously, for 10 minutes until the sugar has completely dissolved. Stir in the tartaric acid (this acts as the preservative and so means that you do not need to sterilize by simmering in a pan of water).

4 Using a slotted spoon, carefully skim off any scum, then transfer the cordial to dry bottles. Seal with airtight tops, then label and leave to cool. Store in a cool, dark place. It will keep for 2–3 months.

5 To serve, dilute 1 part cordial to 4 parts chilled still or sparkling water.

Raspberry and blackberry cordial

Making your own cordials means that you have complete control over what has gone into them. With no artificial colourings or sweeteners, this cordial is as natural as it can be.

MAKES: 2 x 500 ml (17 fl oz) bottles
PREPARATION TIME: 20 minutes, plus straining
COOKING TIME: 2½–2¾ hours

750 g (1½ lb) blackberries
750 g (1½ lb) raspberries
150 ml (¼ pint) water
about 550 g (1 lb 2 oz) granulated sugar

1 Put the fruits into a large bowl and crush with a potato masher. Stir in the water.

2 Set the bowl over a medium pan, one-quarter filled with boiling water, and cook over a low heat for 1 hour.

3 Mash the fruit again, then spoon the mixture into a jelly bag suspended over a large bowl and strain for at least 4 hours or overnight.

4 Measure the cold juice into a large pan and add 375 g (12 oz) sugar for every 600 ml (1 pint) of liquid. Cook over a low heat, stirring continuously, for about 10 minutes until the sugar has completely dissolved.

5 Using a slotted spoon, carefully skim off any scum. Transfer the cordial to warm dry bottles, leaving a headspace of 2.5 cm (1 inch). Add tops and seal loosely.

6 Stand a small wire rack in the bottom of a deep pan and put the bottles, spaced slightly apart, on the rack. Wedge folded pieces of newspaper between the bottles so that they do not fall over or knock together, then fill the pan with cold water to reach the necks of the bottles.

7 Put a sugar thermometer into the pan and slowly heat the water over 1 hour to 77°C (170°F), then maintain the temperature for 20–30 minutes depending on the size of the bottles.

8 Ladle some of the water out of the pan, then, using tongs, carefully lift the bottles out on to a wooden board. Using a cloth, screw the tops on tightly and leave to cool. Label and store in a cool, dark place. The cordial will keep for up to 6 months.

9 To serve, dilute 1 part cordial to 4 parts cold water.

Apple and apricot cordial
Delicately flavoured with just a hint of apricot, this cordial is a good way of using up windfall apples (weigh them after cutting away any bruised or damaged areas).

MAKES: 5 x 250 ml (8 fl oz) bottles
PREPARATION TIME: 30 minutes, plus straining
COOKING TIME: 2½–2¾ hours

2 kg (4 lb) whole, unpeeled cooking apples, roughly chopped
600 ml (1 pint) water
750 g (1½ lb) fresh apricots, quartered and stoned
about 750 g (1½ lb) granulated sugar

1 Put the apples into a bowl of acidulated water (see page 12) as you work so that the flesh does not go brown.

2 Drain the apples, put them into a large pan with the water, cover and bring to the boil. Reduce the heat and simmer, still covered, for 30 minutes until soft.

3 Add the apricots to the apples, cover the pan and cook for 30 minutes until soft.

4 Allow to cool slightly, then strain the mixture for at least 4 hours or overnight through a jelly bag suspended over a large bowl.

5 Measure the cold juice into a large pan and add 375 g (12 oz) sugar for every 600 ml (1 pint) of liquid. Cook over a low heat, stirring continuously, for about 10 minutes until the sugar has completely dissolved. Using a slotted spoon, carefully skim off any scum. Transfer the cordial to warm dry bottles, leaving a headspace of 2.5 cm (1 inch). Add tops and seal loosely.

6 Stand a small wire rack in the bottom of a deep pan and put the bottles, spaced slightly apart, on the rack. Wedge folded pieces of newspaper between the bottles so that they do not fall over or knock together, then fill the pan with cold water to reach the necks of the bottles. Put a sugar thermometer into the pan and slowly heat the water over 1 hour to 77°C (170°F), then maintain the temperature for 20–30 minutes depending on the size of the bottles.

7 Ladle some of the water out of the pan and, using tongs, carefully lift the bottles out on to a wooden board. Using a cloth, screw the tops on tightly and leave to cool overnight. Label and store in a cool, dark place. The cordial will keep for up to 6 months.

8 To serve, dilute 1 part cordial to 4 parts cold water.

Spiced sloe gin
Sloes are only around for a very short time in the autumn. They come from blackthorn trees in the hedgerow and their leaves and fruit look remarkably like those of the olive tree.

MAKES: 750 ml (1¼ pints)

PREPARATION TIME: 15 minutes, plus standing

250 g (8 oz) sloes, stalks removed and soft ones discarded

125 g (4 oz) caster sugar

3 cloves

pared rind of 1 orange

1 cinnamon stick, halved

70 cl bottle of gin

1 Prick each sloe with a fork and drop into a clean dry 1 litre (1¾ pint) wide-necked, screw-topped bottle.

2 Using a plastic funnel or a cone of paper, pour the sugar into the bottle. Stick the cloves into the orange rind and add to the bottle with the halved cinnamon stick.

3 Pour in the gin, seal with an airtight top and turn the bottle upside down two or three times.

4 Stand the bottle in a cool place and turn it once a day for 7 days until the sugar has completely dissolved.

5 Label the bottle and leave to mature in a cool, dark place for 6 months or longer if you can – the longer you leave it the mellower and more delicious it will be. Decant into a serving bottle and discard the sloes. Serve the liqueur in small glasses.

Variation
Damson gin or damson vodka can be made in just the same way, minus the spices, and, unlike the sloes, taste deliciously boozy if spooned on to ice cream.

Tip
• Use the cheapest gin possible for this liqueur as the addition of the sloes, sugar and spices will enhance the gin.

Apricot ratafia
A French-inspired brandy-based liqueur made with fresh apricots and toasted blanched almonds. Add to frangipane tarts or Gâteaux Pithiviers and serve with a glass of the liqueur.

MAKES: 700 ml (24 fl oz)
PREPARATION TIME: 10 minutes, plus standing

50 g (2 oz) blanched almonds, cut into slivers
500 g (1 lb) apricots, quartered and stoned
125 g (4 oz) caster sugar
600 ml (1 pint) brandy

1 Put the almonds on a piece of foil and grill until lightly toasted.

2 Layer the apricots, hot almonds and sugar alternately in a warm dry 1.2 litre (2 pint) wide-necked screw-topped jar.

3 Cover with the brandy, stir the mixture, then screw the lid in place. Leave overnight in a cool, dark place.

4 Gently turn the jar upside down once or twice and repeat this action daily for 4 days until the sugar has completely dissolved.

5 Label the jar and leave to mature in a cool, dark place for a minimum of 3 months. Strain the brandy into a decanter and serve in small liqueur glasses. Serve the apricots and almonds separately topped with cream, crème fraîche or ice cream.

Variation
Use cherries instead of apricots to make cherry ratafia.

Index

Acknowledgements

PHOTOGRAPHY: © **Octopus Publishing Group Ltd**/Stephen Conroy

RECIPE CONTRIBUTION: Sara Lewis
EXECUTIVE EDITOR: Sarah Ford
EDITOR: Alice Bowden
EXECUTIVE ART EDITOR: Leigh Jones
SENIOR PRODUCTION CONTROLLER: Martin Croshaw